seven conversations with
Jorge Luis Borges

··

seven conversations

with

Jorge Luis Borges

FERNANDO SORRENTINO

Translated, with Notes and Appendix
by CLARK M. ZLOTCHEW

PAUL DRY BOOKS
Philadelphia   2010

First Paul Dry Books Edition, 2010

Paul Dry Books, Inc.
Philadelphia, Pennsylvania
www.pauldrybooks.com

1 3 5 7 9 8 6 4 2
Printed in the United States of America

Library of Congress Cataloging-in-Publication Data
Borges, Jorge Luis, 1899–1986.
  [Siete conversaciones con Jorge Luis Borges. English]
  Seven conversations with Jorge Luis Borges / Fernando Sorrentino ;
translated, with Notes and Appendix by Clark M. Zlotchew. —
1st Paul Dry Books ed.
    p. cm.
  Includes indexes.
  Originally published: Troy, N.Y. : Whitston Pub. Co., c1982.
  ISBN 978-1-58988-060-3 (alk. paper)
  1. Borges, Jorge Luis, 1899–1986—Interviews. 2. Authors, Argentine—
20th century—Interviews. I. Sorrentino, Fernando. II. Zlotchew,
Clark M. III. Title.
  PQ7797.B635Z47713 2009
  868—dc22
                                                    2009033107

CONTENTS

Do I contradict myself?
Very well then I contradict myself,
(I am large, I contain multitudes.)
—*Walt Whitman*

Jorge Luis Borges is the most eminent Latin-American writer of the twentieth century. It is even safe to say that he is the best known and most admired living writer in the Spanish language. Translated into all the major tongues, his poetry, essays, and short fiction are among the most important pieces of modern world literature. Very few authors are as widely praised, criticized, loved, abhorred, discussed, or argued over. A respected critic and novelist has described him in these contradictory terms: "arbitrary, brilliant, tender, precise, weak, great, triumphant, daring, timid, a failure, magnificent, wretched, limited, infantile, immortal."[1] To say any more about Borges within the confines of these introductory pages would be to say too much and, at the same time, to say too little. Too much because his fame would make redundant any catalog of his accomplishments. Too little because the detailed critical and philosophical discussion his work gives rise to would be far beyond the scope of a foreword to a series of conversations in which Borges speaks for himself.

These dialogues with Borges have been called the best book of its kind, the one that provides the most reliable picture of Borges derived from tape-recorded conversations with him. The same critic finds in these interviews an exceptionally open and intimate tone.[2] The conversations were recorded on tape in 1972 and published in 1974 in Argentina but, because of the overly frank tone of Borges' political statements, could not be commercially distributed until after the overthrow of Isabel Perón in 1976.

Fernando Sorrentino is Borges' interviewer in these pages. Born in 1942, this young Argentinean writer is an author of fiction in his own right as well as a devoted anthologist of Spanish-American short stories and an instructor of literature in the secondary schools of Buenos Aires. His literary production (consisting of over thirty short stories published in various newspapers, three books of short stories, a collection of juvenile stories, and a novel) is predominantly satirical in nature, ranging from the dryly ironic—at times sardonic—observation of human foibles to the frankly hilarious exaggeration of normal situations to the point in which they take on alarming proportions which approach the surreal. Sorrentino's novel, *Sanitarios centenarios* (Buenos Aires: Plus Ultra, 1979), concerning the advertising campaign mounted on behalf of a bathroom fixture firm celebrating its hundredth anniversary, is a satire involving the delusions of grandeur of ordinary people; it is also an uproariously funny narrative.[3]

A series of interviews even with the most talented author can result in a bleak succession of banalities that prove to be a disappointment for the avid fan; a great deal depends on the skill of the interviewer. Fernando Sorrentino is endowed with literary acumen, sensitivity, urbanity, a familiarity with Borges' work, and the ability to allow Borges to roam freely over unsuspected paths while at the same time maintaining a firm control over the direction taken by the conversation. All these qualities are as responsible for this warm and personal glimpse of one of the most fascinating figures in contemporary world literature as Borges' own personality is.

Borges wanders from nostalgic reminiscence to literary criticism and from philosophical speculation to political pronouncements. His thoughts on literature alone run the gamut from the Bible and Homer to Hemingway and Cortázar. We learn that Dante is the writer who has impressed Borges most, that Borges considers García Lorca to be a "second-rate poet," and that he feels Bioy Casares is one of the most important authors of this century. Borges dwells lovingly on Buenos Aires, too.

As in his prose and more often in his poetry, in these pages Borges refers to the outskirts of the City and to the denizens of those humble quarters. In those frequent references, he speaks of a Buenos Aires which essentially no longer exists. The fact that the Buenos Aires of Borges' youth bears much less resemblance to a North American city than does the Argentine Capital of today (the city Borges has not seen—through blindness—for a quarter of a century) makes it difficult to translate some of the terms he employs when commenting on the Buenos Aires of old.

The term *suburbio* literally denotes "suburb," deriving from the same Latin *sub* and *urbs* as does the English word. But here the similarity ends. When the North American thinks of suburbs, he thinks of two-car garages, manicured lawns, country clubs, good schools—in other words: affluence. The Latin-American *suburbio* is typically a marginal zone, both literally and figuratively: a zone on the edges of society. It is the poorer quarters huddled on the cheaper land at the outskirts of the big city where destitute country folk settle hoping to find a better life. An entire sub-culture develops in these suburbs characterized by poverty and the cult of violence and *machismo*. In this respect, the Latin-American *suburb* is practically synonymous with the North American "slum" or "inner city"; yet, like the Northern affluent suburb, it is situated around the fringes of the city. The situations are reversed, making a simple one-word translation unfeasible. In the text of this English version, the term *suburb*, because of the peculiar connotations it has for the North American, is avoided. Instead, expressions such as "outlying slums," "outer limits," "less affluent fringe areas," and the like are employed.

When referring to the inhabitants of these zones of Buenos Aires and their peculiar lifestyle, Borges uses the words *compadre*, *compadrito*, *orillero*, and *malevo*. There is no exact English equivalent for any of them. At the end of the nineteenth century, the *compadre* was a man who earned his livelihood, whether in the country or on the outskirts of Buenos Aires, either as a cart driver, cattle drover, or animal slaughterer.[4] The *compadre* might be thought of as an urbanized (or semi-urbanized) gaucho. Many of the traits of the gaucho—self-assurance, courage, love of personal freedom and of being footloose—were typical of the *compadre*.

The *compadrito* (diminutive of *compadre*) was the young man of the *suburbios* whose only interests were women, dancing, guitar playing, and drinking the local rum called *caña*. He customarily lived at his woman's expense. He differed from the *compadre* mainly in his youth and his avoidance of work. By extension, the term *compadrito* came to include the young men who liked to imitate the attitudes and flashy dress of the genuine article. Toward the 1880s many *compadritos* became out-and-out pimps. (The slang term for pimps as such was *canfinfleros* or *cafishos*.) They would exploit only one woman (unlike the pimp of the North American inner city who maintains an entire "stable") or two, at most, who would work in a house of prostitution for the *cafisho*. The *compadrito* could be quarrelsome and *macho* but not necessarily as aggressive as the *guapo* or the *malevo*.

The *guapo* was the *compadre* or *compadrito* who was aggressively brave. He enjoyed imposing his will on others and insisted on being respected and obeyed. Generally, he was employed as a bodyguard by a local political boss; this fact guaranteed him impunity for any killings imputed to him after a knife fight.

The *malevo* (apparently the short form of *malévolo*, "malevolent") was the *guapo* with a mean streak. He would pick a quarrel for the mere pleasure of fighting. He could be a murderer if the opportunity presented itself and, at times, a thief.

The generic term for all the above types was *orillero*, that is, inhabitant of the *orillas* (literally "sea shore" or "river bank" but by extension in Buenos Aires: "edges of town" and therefore "slums"). Obviously, no strict classification is possible in practice; it would be difficult to say that one man is a pure *guapo* while another is a *compadrito* or a *malevo*. The categories were usually overlapping. In some novels depicting more recent times, the *compadrito* is presented as nothing more than a poor, ignorant young man who has nothing to do but loaf around the *suburbio*, a sort of "drugstore cowboy." It is not difficult to see that the meaning of these terms has changed through the years and cannot be rendered precisely.

The average Argentinean of today has only a vague understanding of the above terms; only the specialist in Buenos Aires history or the philologist specializing in Buenos Aires slang has a clear idea of this nomenclature. It is difficult to know how accurate Borges' use of these terms is. In any case, his terms referring to the types who lived in the *suburbios* during his childhood have here been translated, depending on context, variously as *dudes, toughs, hoodlums, bully boys, idlers*, and *drugstore cowboys*, while in another context the term *compadre* was retained.

Perhaps it would be wise to state that today's Buenos Aires bears little resemblance to that of Borges' youth. Whereas the outer fringes of many Latin-American cities are still poverty-ridden hotbeds of violence and crime, Buenos Aires has assimilated the marginal elements to a great extent. The world Borges nostalgically refers to—a world of corner saloons painted pink or blue, men dancing the tango in the street with each other (no woman would be seen dancing the "shameful" tango), knife fights—is a world which no longer exists. For example, at the southern rim of the Capital is the city of Avellaneda, an industrial suburb (i.e. a satellite of the metropolis) of Buenos Aires filled with factories and packing houses. The population is predominantly working class, but doctors, lawyers, engineers, and other professionals live there as well. On the other hand, there is a string of beautiful residential towns with luxurious homes with swimming pools and parks with shade trees on the northern fringes of the Capital. These too are suburbs, and just as in the United States and in Canada, they are inhabited mainly by members of the upper middle class as well as by those who are decidedly upper class. Nevertheless, there are bakers, butchers, storekeepers, and others of the lower middle class living there too. The *compadrito* and his ilk have vanished just as the gaucho had done in an earlier epoch.

Most of the detailed information on the inhabitants of the *suburbios* of old has been graciously furnished by don José Gobello, that highly esteemed etymologist, lexicologist, specialist in Lunfardo (Buenos Aires slang), and authority on tango lyrics. A special note of thanks is extended to him for his patient and courteous response to my queries. Gratitude is also due Fernando Sorrentino himself who has spent a great deal of time and energy guiding me over the rough spots. The notes for this English-language edition have been greatly expanded and otherwise modified for the convenience of the North American public; Sorrentino has been extremely cooperative in working with me on those notes with respect to Argentinean data. An appendix has been added to this English version in order to provide information on personalities of the Hispanic world mentioned by Borges. For their aid in tracing citations from British and North American literature or for providing cinematographic information, I thank Mr. Gary Barber, Mr. John Moran, Ms. Margaret Pabst, and Mrs. Franciska Safran of the Reed Library (S. U. C. Fredonia), Professors Robert Schweik, George Sebouhian, James Shokoff, and John Stinson of the State University of New York, College at Fredonia, and Professor Richard J. A. Kerr of the State University of New York at Binghamton. I thank Ms. Marie Zambotti for her help in preparing the manuscript, and my wife Marilyn for telling me when a particular phrase was more Spanish than English.

Clark M. Zlotchew
Fredonia, N.Y.
June 1980

Addendum

Jorge Luis Borges was still writing when my 1982 English version of Fernando Sorrentino's interviews with him was published. I had been fascinated with Borges' writing since I first read him in 1963 and was glad to have the opportunity to translate these conversations. Borges died in 1986 after having added much more to his literary production, but I had the opportunity to meet him in person before then. I interviewed him in Buenos Aires in 1984, and I had several conversations with him at Allegheny College in Meadville, Pennsylvania, in 1985. As a result, when I read any interview with him or any of his fictions, in my "mind's ear" I can actually hear him speaking.

The enormous importance of Jorge Luis Borges to the literary world and the reading public has not changed since the 1982 translation was published. Fernando Sorrentino, Borges' astute and informed interviewer, himself a man of letters, has added to his own literary output. Over one hundred of his short stories have appeared in magazines, newspapers, and on the Internet in the original Spanish as well as in a host of languages throughout the world, from English and Polish to Vietnamese and Chinese. Sorrentino has had twenty-seven books published in his original Spanish: short story collections, stories for children and adolescents, two books of interviews, a novel, and a novella. Abundant information on Sorrentino's literary production can be found at http://fernandosorrentino.com.ar.

Sorrentino has had several editions of these dialogues published in Spanish, adding more notes to each one. In my translation of 1982 I had multiplied the notes to cover matters that the average English-speaker would not know. I have included both my additional notes of 1982 and Sorrentino's copious newer notes (in my translation) for this Paul Dry Books edition.

Clark M. Zlotchew
Fredonia, N.Y.
June 2009

Paradoxically, the dialogues which take place between a writer and a journalist bear less resemblance to a question-and-answer session than to a kind of introspection. For the interviewer, they can be a chore which is not entirely free of fatigue and tedium; for the interviewee, they are like an adventure in which the hidden and the unforeseeable lie in wait. Fernando Sorrentino knows my work—let us use that term—much better than I do; this is due to the obvious fact that I have written it one single time and he has read it many times, a fact which makes it less mine than his. As I dictate these lines, I do not wish to slight his kindly perspicacity: how many afternoons, speaking face to face, has he guided me, as though it were unintentional, to the inevitable answers which later astonished me and which he, no doubt, had prepared.

Fernando Sorrentino is, in a word, one of my most generous inventors. I wish to take advantage of this page to tell him of my gratitude and the certainty of a friendship that will not be erased by the years.

Jorge Luis Borges
Buenos Aires
July 13, 1972

I first spoke with Jorge Luis Borges—I made certain to jot down the date—that broiling afternoon of December 2, 1968. I was on my way to work—gloomily, as befits the situation. As luck would have it, Borges emerged from Moreno Station on to the broad, landscaped traffic island that divides Nueve de Julio Avenue. I greeted him excitedly, awkwardly; I sputtered my name, a name unknown to him. I told him I lived in the Palermo district. This pleased him, and a moment later we were talking about Maldonado Creek, a "creek" which to my eyes had never been anything other than a long stretch of gray asphalt flanked by an elevated train and many wine storehouses. I recall that I recited the first few stanzas of his poem "El tango," and that Borges reproached me: "What a waste of time reading those things!"

Many months later I had an opportunity to converse at length with Borges.[1] For seven afternoons, the teller of tales preceded me, opening tall doors which revealed unsuspected spiral staircases, through the National Library's pleasant maze of corridors, in search of a secluded little room where we would not be interrupted by the telephone.

These seven conversations were tape recorded and then set down on paper. The Borges who speaks to us in this book is a courteous, easy-going gentleman who verifies no quotations, who does not look back to correct mistakes, who pretends to have a poor memory; he is not the terse Jorge Luis Borges of the printed page, that Borges who calculates and measures each comma and each parenthesis. The heterogeneity and disorder which plague the questions have as their aim to make of this book something other than an organic essay, to make it exactly that which its title declares: seven low-key, casual chats, free from any bothersome adherence to a rigid format. As a result of this lack of self-consciousness, there are repetitions here and there, certain ambiguities, and a few sentences suffering from what the art of rhetoric designates *anacoluthon*. Inevitably, someone will deplore the absence of questions on Gracián; someone else will have had recourse to the book with the exclusive purpose of learning something about Molière. Yet another will be indignant to note that no mention is made of Hermann Hesse.

I have tried to be as unfastidious as possible in the notes. Their only purpose is to place Jorge Luis Borges within his literary and political context.[2] It is true that the reader can, with no great loss, do without them.

Fernando Sorrentino
Buenos Aires
July 1972

PROLOGUE

... I judge literature in a Hedonistic fashion. That is, I judge literature according to the pleasure or emotion it produces in me.
—*J. L. B.*

When I conducted the series of seven interviews with Jorge Luis Borges, I had not yet reached the age of thirty. I was animated by unlimited energy, optimism, and enthusiasm and by the certainty of being able to achieve any sensible objective I set for myself. I found myself in those happy circumstances around the year 1970.

Now, I've been alive for more than a half century, my energy and enthusiasm quite diminished, my optimism seriously reduced. Consequently, I entertain more modest ideas concerning my ability to accomplish objectives of any type at all.

From the time I first learned how to read, I became a sort of literature addict and, most especially, an addict of narrative literature. I love to be told stories and for those stories to be—in the best sense of the word—*interesting*. For that very reason, it never seemed praiseworthy to me to read unpleasant, dull, or boring books, nor to read them because of some categorical imperative. I have attempted, unsuccessfully, to admire both the altruistic writers who produce best sellers and the egoists who entangle themselves in unreadable texts.

With this pleasure-seeking attitude, I simply gave myself over to reading. I read what I liked and dropped what bored me. And, as the years passed, I began to notice a process of decantation. I determined that some books required no second reading; that some books wearied and irritated me right from the beginning; that with other books, I would be forgetting them at the same time I was reading them; that through the syntax and the vocabulary of still other books, I could see the laughably serious faces of their authors portrayed; that still other books existed only in the print media and in recreational writing clubs where similarly-minded people read (and praised) each other's work, but not in the world of actual literature. Etc., etc., etc.

Luckily, I also found very good friends in so many books. Friends who never bored me or disappointed me and to whose works—in a kind of insatiable love affair—I would return time and time again, always finding new riches and new wonders.

One of those dear friends is, of course, Borges. That's how I felt when, in 1961 for the very first time I read his work (the short stories of *Ficciones*). At that moment, fascinated, I experienced the sensation of being faced with a unique kind of magic literature, a kind of literature completely unparalleled and which, therefore, was *incomparable*, in the most literal sense.

This is how I felt in 1961; this is how I still feel—only more so—thirty-five long years later. My readings of Borges have been always spontaneous, always repeated, always pleasurable. In a world in which we all receive, as well as bestow, good things and bad things, my overriding feeling toward Borges is gratitude for all the good that he gave me and continues to give me.

Twenty-five years ago I asked him the questions that were provided to me—as to all mortals—by the alliance between curiosity and chance. Had I interviewed him years later, my questions, in general, would have been more or less the same, excluding, however, those which did not stir his interest—there were just a few of these—but adding others that would have given free rein to his unforeseeable flow of ideas (which were at various times on the mark, erroneous, reasonable, irritating, puerile, benevolent, or cruel, but always intelligent).

As would be expected, the interviews are here reproduced without modification, with respect to the previous edition, except for the elimination of errata. On the other hand, I have added, eliminated, and reworked notes, at times by correcting erroneous information, at times by trying to be more precise about the data, without these efforts meaning that the task has been completed.

I owe a debt of gratitude to Miguel de Torre, a devotee of his illustrious uncle, for his generosity with not only accurate genealogical and family data on Borges, but for his many intelligent observations as well.

I have been able to enrich some references to the culture of the English-speaking world by making good use of the notes added to the first English edition by the translator, Clark M. Zlotchew.

Borges passed away on June 14, 1986. It is no longer possible to indulge in further interviews:* an undoubtedly minor literary genre, at any rate.

But here they are, and forever, the inexhaustible words of *Ficciones* and *El Aleph* and of *El informe de Brodie* and of *El libro de arena*, and those of so many other beloved pages, without which—to use a phrase often employed by Borges—this world would be so much the poorer.

F. S.
Buenos Aires
May 1996

---

*In his "Prologue" Borges refers to me as a "journalist," a profession I have never practiced and which, God willing, I never will practice.

seven conversations with
Jorge Luis Borges

first
conversation

The Turtle in the Well — The Assassination of Ricardo López
Jordán — The Limits of Buenos Aires — The English Grandmother
— Poems to the Russian Revolution — The Florida/Boedo Hoax
— Origins of the Tango — Lugones and the Errors of Ultraism —
The Timelessness of Banchs — Macedonio Fernández and Xul Solar
— Leopoldo Marechal — Güiraldes, Amorim, and the Gauchos —
Roberto Arlt's Subtlety — Américo Castro's Prophecy — Francisco
de Quevedo, Peronist — Paul Groussac's Affability

FERNANDO SORRENTINO   When and where was Jorge Luis
Borges born?

JORGE LUIS BORGES   I was born on August 24, 1899.[1] I'm
happy about this because I like the nineteenth century very
much, although it could be said to the detriment of the nineteenth century that it led to the twentieth century, which I
find less admirable. I was born on Tucumán Street[2] between
Esmeralda and Suipacha, and I know that all the houses on the
block were one-story affairs except for the combination gro-
cery-saloon, which had a second story, and every house was
constructed in the style of the Argentine Society of Writers,[3]
except that the house in which I was born was much more modest. That is, it had two windows with iron grillwork, the door
to the street with its ring-shaped knocker, then the vestibule,
next the inner door, then the rooms, the side courtyard, and
the well. And in the bottom of the well—I found this out much
later—there was a turtle for purifying the water. So my grandparents, my parents, and I had drunk turtle water for years and
it hadn't done us any harm; nowadays it would disgust us to
think we're drinking turtle water. My mother remembers hav-

ing heard as a little girl—besides the bullets of the 1890 Revolution—one exceptional bullet: my grandfather went out and said General Ricardo López Jordán had been assassinated right around the corner. Some people say the assassin, under contract with the Urquiza family, provoked and then killed him. I believe this is false. Actually, López Jordán had had this man's father killed, so this fellow picked a quarrel with López Jordán, killed him with one shot, fled down Tucumán Street and was captured after he had made it to Florida Street.

F.S. At that time, where did the built-up portion of the City end?

J.L.B. I can give you two answers. Formerly, the City ended at Centro América Street—that is, [today's] Pueyrredón. Mother remembers this. But my mother is ninety-five years old. Beyond that point there were vacant lots, country homes, brick kilns, a large lagoon, clusters of shacks, people riding on horseback, inhabitants of the outlying slums. But when I was a child we moved to the Palermo district, which was at one end of the City, and at that time the buildings ended precisely at the Pacífico Bridge, on Maldonado Creek, where the Paloma Café still stands, I believe.

F.S. Used to stand: there's a pizzeria there now.[4]

J.L.B. Everything is going to the dogs! They used to have *truco* [a card game] competitions there. And then there were no more buildings up to the Belgrano district, let's say somewhere around Federico Lacroze Street, I suppose. But in all that space there were a great many vacant lots. Maldonado Creek apparently gave rise to bad neighborhoods no matter where—the Palermo district, or Villa Crespo, or Flores—neighborhoods of prostitution, of hoodlums.

F.S. Is that where your "Hombre de la esquina rosada" (Streetcorner Man) takes place?

J.L.B. Yes, but a little further out. I had it take place beyond Flores and gave it an indeterminate date. I did it deliberately. I believe that a writer should never attempt a contemporary theme or a very precise topography. Otherwise people are immediately going to find mistakes. Or if they don't find them, they're going to look for them, and if they look for them, they'll find them. That's why I prefer to have my stories take place in somewhat indeterminate places and many years ago. For example, the best story I've ever written, "La intrusa" (The Intruder), takes place in Turdera, on the outskirts of Adrogué or of Lomas; it takes place more or less at the end of the last century or at the beginning of this one. And I did it deliberately so no one could say to me: "No, people aren't like that." The other day I came upon a young fellow who told me he was going to write a novel about a café called "El Socorrito," at the corner of Juncal and Esmeralda:[5] a contemporary novel. I told him not to say the café was "El Socorrito" and not to say the time is the present, because if he did someone was going to tell him: "The people in that café don't talk that way" or "The atmosphere is phony." So I think a certain distance in time and space is appropriate. Besides, I believe that the idea that literature should treat contemporary themes is relatively new. If I'm not mistaken, the *Iliad* was probably written two or three centuries after the fall of Troy. I think that freedom of imagination demands that we search for subjects which are distant in time or in space, or if not, on other planets, the way those who write science-fiction are doing right now. Otherwise, we are somewhat tied down by reality, and literature already seems too much like journalism.

F.S. Do you mean you don't believe in psychological literature somehow?

J.L.B. Yes, of course I believe in psychological literature, and I think that all literature is fundamentally psychological. The acts performed by a character are facets of or ways of describing that character. Juan Ramón Jiménez said he could imagine a *Don Quixote* with adventures other than those contained in the book.[6] I believe that what is important in *Don Quixote* are the characters possessed by Alonso Quijano and

Sancho [Panza]. But we can imagine other fictional events. Cervantes was aware of that fact when he wrote the second part, which I think is far superior to the first. What doesn't seem right to me is for literature to become confused with journalism or with history. It appears to me that literature should be psychological and should be imaginative. I, at least when I'm alone, tend to think and to imagine. But I wouldn't be able to tell you—of course my being practically blind enters into it—the number of chairs there are in this room. And maybe you could do it now only if you were to count them.

F.S. When and where did you learn to read?

J.L.B. I don't remember a time in which I didn't know how to read, which means I learned very early.

F.S. Did you learn in English or in Spanish first?

J.L.B. In Spanish, of course.[7] Although one language was spoken as much as the other in our house. Mother always jokes with my sister and me. She calls us "quadroons." Because she's of old-line Argentinean stock and my paternal grandmother was English, but an Englishwoman who knew the country better than many Argentineans because my grandfather, Colonel Borges,[8] was Commander of the Three Frontiers: that is to say, of the North and West of Buenos Aires Province and the South of Santa Fe, after having taken part in the Great War, in Uruguay, in the Uruguayan division that took Palomar in the battle of Caseros, in Leones Canyon, on the Azul, in the Paraguayan War, against López Jordán's gaucho cavalry . . . That English grandmother of mine lived for four years in Junín, which is to say the end of the world, because beyond Junín was what used to be called "out back," which was Indian country. The Indians were especially prevalent in the town called Los Toldos (The Wigwams)—near Junín—and it was called Los Toldos because that's where the Indian camp was. And my grandmother told me she had spoken with Simón Coliqueo, with Catriel, with someone or other of the Curá [dynasty of chiefs].

F.S. In *El Aleph* there's a story of yours which deals with an Englishwoman who had lived among the Indians.[9]

J.L.B. Yes, that's right; my grandmother told me that one. I haven't added a thing to it. When I began to write, I thought, no doubt under the influence of so many nineteenth-century novelists, that I had to document myself carefully. And now, conversely, I think that the less I intervene in what I write, the better. That is, if I've been told a story, and if that story has impressed me, it's better to tell it exactly as I heard it rather than to look up details in books. I believe that here too it's my laziness that is speaking and the fact that since I can't see, I would have to make it difficult for others to document me. But I believe that a brief short story, like the first short stories written by Kipling, can be highly charged and very effective and nevertheless not exceed a dozen pages.

F.S. Of course; you even maintain that stories exactly as they come, polished by time, are the best.

J.L.B. Yes, that's why I think that each year a person hears four or five anecdotes that are very good, precisely because they've been worked on. Because it's wrong to suppose that the fact that they're anonymous means they haven't been worked on. On the contrary, I think fairy tales, legends, even the off-color jokes one hears, are usually good because having been passed from mouth to mouth, they've been stripped of everything that might be useless or bothersome. So we could say that a folk tale is a much more refined product than a poem by Donne or by Góngora or by Lugones, for example, since in the second case the piece has been refined by a single person, and in the first case by hundreds.

F.S. In those early years of your life, you went off, I believe, to Europe, to Switzerland.

J.L.B. To Switzerland. To Geneva, a city I love very much, one of the several homelands I have. What might they be? Buenos Aires: the Palermo district where I grew up;[10] the

South Side, which I always loved so much; and then I think of Geneva, which is a part of those important years of puberty and adolescence. And cities I've been in a couple of days and love very much: Edinburgh, for instance, or Copenhagen, or Santiago de Compostela in Spain. It's strange that geographically modest places have impressed me most. I spent ten days in the border town of Rivera [in Uruguay], which has a Brazilian side called Sant' Anna do Livramento; I went with Enrique Amorim. And I see that in my stories I tend to recall those ten days[11] I spent in Sant' Anna do Livramento and where I certainly experienced something that impressed me: a few steps away from me a man was shot to death.

F.S. In 1918 you were in Lugano, isn't that so?

J.L.B. Yes, and I remember that we were crossing the square with my father. Father said to me: "Let's see what that blackboard (of some newspaper or other) says." The blackboard reported the news—already expected, of course—that the Germans had surrendered. We went to the hotel and Father told the news to Mother. We said: "How lucky, the war has ended, ended in victory."

F.S. And around that time the Communist Revolution took place in Russia.

J.L.B. That's right, and I wrote poems dedicated to the Russian Revolution,[12] which of course hasn't anything to do with present-day Soviet imperialism. We saw the Russian Revolution as a sort of beginning for peace among all men. My father was an anarchist, a Spencerian, a reader of *The Man Versus the State*, and I recall that in one of the long summer vacations we took in Montevideo, my father told me to take a good look at many things because those things were going to disappear and I would be able to tell my children or grandchildren—I haven't had any children or grandchildren—that I had seen those things. He told me to look at military barracks, flags, maps having different colors for the different countries, butcher shops, churches, priests, customs houses, because all of those things were going to disappear when the world was one and differences were forgotten. Up until now the prophecy hasn't come true, but I hope it will come true some day. But I want to reiterate that I saw the Russian Revolution as the beginning of peace among all men, as something which has nothing to do with present-day Soviet imperialism.

F.S. I understand that those poems haven't been collected in book form.

J.L.B. I destroyed those poems because they were very bad anyway.

F.S. And you were eighteen or nineteen years old.

J.L.B. Yes and I was trying to be modern, and wanted to be an Expressionist poet. I no longer believe in literary schools now; I believe in the individual.

F.S. In 1919 you were in Spain and were one of the Ultraists.

J.L.B. Yes, that group was founded by Rafael Cansinos Assens and I realized that he had done it somewhat ironically. It was somewhat of a joke like the Florida and Boedo polemics, for example, which I see is now taken seriously, but—doubtlessly Marechal must have said it already[13]—there were no such polemics or such groups or anything. All that was organized by Ernesto Palacio and Roberto Mariani. They thought about the literary cliques in Paris and thought it might be useful as publicity if there were two inimical, hostile groups. So the two groups were formed. At that time I was writing poetry about the outer fringes of Buenos Aires, those poorer neighborhoods at the edges of the City. So I asked: "What are the two groups?" "Florida and Boedo," they told me. I had never heard anyone mention Boedo Street even though I was living on Bulnes,[14] an extension of Boedo. "Well," I said, "and what do they represent?" "Florida represents the downtown area and Boedo would be the outskirts." "Well," I told them, "sign me up with the Boedo group." "It's too late; you're already in the Florida group." "Well," I said, "after all, how important is topography?" The proof of the matter is, for instance, the fact that a writer like Arlt belonged to both groups; a writer like Olivari, too. We never took all that business seriously. On the other hand, I see that it's being taken seriously now, and they're even giving examinations on it. No doubt Marechal must have said all this.

F.S. Marechal said that those two groups were based more on lifestyle than on literature because, according to him, the fact that Oliverio Girondo directed traffic at Callao and Corrientes was more important than what he was writing.

J.L.B. The fact is that Oliverio Girondo never counted for much as a writer. Oliverio Girondo financed the *Martín Fierro* review, but his own personal work . . . I don't think he felt it to be important either. I think he was more interested in typography, in printing. What did he actually write? Witty aphorisms, more or less. In short . . . I don't know: he wasn't an important poet like Horacio Rega Molina, let's say, or like Norah Lange. Norah Lange wrote a book, *Cuadernos de infancia* (Childhood Notebook), which is really a beautiful book! Memories of the Province of Mendoza. Oliverio took it as a kind of joke, too. Oliverio had lived in Paris for a long time. I think that he, like Güiraldes, was one of those young socialites who brought the tango to Paris and who got the people of Buenos Aires to accept it. Because the people of Buenos Aires didn't want to accept the tango. As a child—and I grew up in a poor neighborhood, in the Palermo district, Carriego's neighborhood—I saw the tango danced with all the dips and breaks by the men who used to hang out on street corners. Because no woman would be caught doing it; they knew it was a dance with the worst kind of reputation: what Lugones had referred to as a "brothel snake." But when they learned it was being danced by the pillars of society, the people resigned themselves and danced it, but there was a great deal of resistance to the tango among the people because they saw it as a dance connected with the scum of the earth. But it used to be very different, because it used to be a merry dance, very lively, with . . . to be frank, obscene movements. In Paris it was cleaned up a great deal; it was made into something sad, and then some people came along who even took it upon themselves to change it. "La cumparsita," for example, already reflects that change. Gardel too, who has no connection with the old style of singing the tango. I've been interested in the origins of the tango. I've spoken with Saborido, the composer of "La morocha" and of "Felicia." I've spoken with Ernesto Ponzio, composer of "El entrerriano" and, I believe, of "Don Juan."[15] I've spoken with Nicolás Paredes, who was a political boss in the Palermo district. I've spoken with an uncle of mine who was a playboy and a rake. I've spoken with people from Montevideo, from Rosario. And with Marcelo del Mazo too. And they've all given me the same origin. The topography varies because, naturally, in Rosario they like to suppose it's Rosarian; in Montevideo, that it's Montevidean; in Buenos Aires, that it's Buenos Airean. But in any case the origin is identical: the houses of ill repute. That is, it didn't originate with the people, either. It arose out of that mixed ambience of rakish young aristocrats and pimps. And this can be demonstrated, as I've written more than once—but I can repeat it for a book like this—through the instruments. If the tango had been of the people, a folk dance, then the instrument would have been the guitar, which is what one used to hear in all the old-time grocery store-saloons previously. Not the piano, flute, and violin, which are more expensive instruments. And later they added the concertina. And later, this time in the Boca district—an almost exclusively Genoese neighborhood, of course—they made the tango very sentimental: "Italian," in the lachrymose sense of the word. But the origin can be seen in the instruments. And we have this in Marcelo del Mazo's poem:[16]

> When the rhythm of that tango marked a hesitation beat,
> like serpents animated by a vapor of passion,
> they entwined . . . And they were the stems of a strange vine
> blooming in the rain of comments in the dance hall.

"Now, baby!", howled the dude, and his sullen partner
offered the impudence of her torrid immodesty.
Arousing, with her flesh like tongues of flame,
the quivering entrails of that lowlife of love.

(By "lowlife of love" meaning "that pimp," right?)

Around and around they spun; the violins went wild
and the flute hit some notes that no one ever wrote.
But the dancers moved along smoothly, without missing a beat,
and slowly, without realizing it, the two of them kissed. . . .

You see: flute and violin. If the tango had been of the people, the instrument would have been the guitar, which was the instrument of the *milonga* and the *estilo*. However, I don't think the guitar was ever used; or maybe it has been used lately. The concertina came much later, of course.

F.S. When you were writing your first poems and Lugones was alive, what did he think of your poetry?

J.L.B. He didn't like it at all. And I believe he was entirely correct. But at the same time, there was something more important for me: I think he held me in high regard as a person, and that's much more important, isn't it?[17] And the proof of this is that I allowed myself a few unpardonably impertinent remarks about him.[18] I think part of the reason I did it was to free myself from Lugones' gravitational field; it's the same story with everyone of my generation. So we indulged in the childishness of saying that poetry consisted of one essential element: metaphor. That must have been around 1925, let's say. And we were forgetting that Lugones had done exactly the same thing and had regretted it, and that he had invented better metaphors than we as far back as 1909 in *Lunario sentimental* (Sentimental Moon Calendar), where he adds two elements: new meter and varied rhyme. In general, I don't believe in any school which starts by impoverishing things. And I believe Ultraism's error—except that Ultraism is of no importance—was that of not having enriched, of having simply forbidden. For example: we, almost all of us, were writing without punctuation marks. It would have been much more interesting to invent new punctuation marks, that is, to *enrich* literature. Reducing literature to the metaphor . . . But why the metaphor? The metaphor is just one of so many rhetorical devices; then again it was already defined by Aristotle, etc. I think one of Ultraism's errors was wanting to start a revolution by impoverishing art. It would have been better had we invented new punctuation marks, something we could have done easily. Or maybe not easily, but we could have attempted it. On the other hand, ours was a revolution that consisted of what?: of relegating literature to a single device, the metaphor. Lugones had already done that and had regretted doing it. I recall that we all devoted ourselves to writing poems about the moon and about the close of day, no doubt influenced by Lugones. And once the poem was written, we would look in Lugones' text, the *Lunario*, and there was our metaphor expressed better than we had expressed it. And Lugones' influence is noticeable throughout the Movement. A book I admire, *Don Segundo Sombra*, is a book which is inconceivable without the existence of Lugones' *El payador* (The Gaucho Troubadour), since they more or less share the same style, the same type of metaphors and images. But I imagine Marechal must have said all this.

F.S. He spoke of something similar: a polemic he had with Lugones and . . .

J.L.B. But I suppose the polemic was probably unilateral, because I don't think Lugones would be aware of the existence of that kind of polemic.

F.S. Marechal says that he sang his *mea culpa* when he dedicated his *Laberinto de amor* (Labyrinth of Love), to him, respecting all the principles of meter and rhyme in it, but that Lugones didn't even trouble to answer him.[19]

J.L.B. You see, Lugones couldn't be interested in a revolution composed of his own echoes, echoes which he had regretted, because after all, the *Lunario sentimental* does not exhaust Lugones' work: there are the *Odas seculares* (Secular Odes), *Las horas doradas* (The Gilded Hours); there's that book of fantastic stories, *Las fuerzas extrañas* (Strange Forces); there's that *Historia de Sarmiento* (History of Sarmiento); there's *El payador*, which is a kind of re-creation of *Martín Fierro*.

F.S. And you Ultraists, how did you feel about a somewhat earlier poet, someone like Enrique Banchs?

J.L.B. We considered him a great poet! How could we possibly feel any other way about him? Why, we knew his poems by heart!

F.S. Then why did you attack Lugones and not Banchs when Banchs was, at least with respect to meter, a classicist?

J.L.B. The two cases were entirely different. Lugones was a man with a powerful personality. On the other hand, Banchs, perhaps being a greater poet than Lugones—if poets can really be compared—is a poet who can be defined only by perfection. Lugones had an influence on his contemporaries, had an influence on his successors; a great poet like Ezequiel Martínez Estrada would be inconceivable without Lugones and without Darío. On the other hand, the work of Banchs—although somewhat reflecting the Modernist Movement—is a work which has exerted no influence whatsoever. I mean to say: if *La urna* (The Urn) didn't exist—because Banchs' other books don't seem important to me: *Las barcas* (The Boats), *El cascabel del halcón* (Falcon Bell), *El libro de los elogios* (The Book of Eulogies), and even less so his prose—the world would be the poorer because we would have missed the beauty of those sonnets. Because those sonnets are nothing less than perfect. This is so true that it's very easy—no, not very easy, it's possible—to do a parody of Lugones, but I don't believe it possible to do a parody of Banchs. Because Banchs is a poet who doesn't have a style in the sense of a particular vocabulary: Banchs' nightingales, or afternoons, or solitude, are themes that belong to all of lyric poetry, to elegiac poetry. On the other hand—I'm going to use the humblest of examples—I think it's very easy to do a parody of me, and I devote myself to doing that, because everyone knows that what I write is a repertory of games with time, of mirrors, of labyrinths, of daggers, of masks.

F.S. And of drugstore cowboys and heresiarchs.

J.L.B. And of drugstore cowboys and heresiarchs, as Ernesto Sábato said.[20] On the other hand, what do we have in Banchs? We have a man who, as luck would have it, was not loved by a particular woman in 1911. And that personal misfortune has left us *La urna*, which is quite something to leave. So we viewed Banchs as being timeless. He was a poet we loved very much, and to write anything against him would have been as absurd as to write against Keats or against Garcilaso. It wouldn't have made sense.

F.S. Since you've talked about parodies, did you read "Homicidio filosófico"[21] (Philosophical Homicide), that story in which Conrado Nalé Roxlo writes in the style of Jorge Luis Borges?

J.L.B. No, I haven't read that parody. Anyway, I don't like parodies. Lugones said: "Parody, an intrinsically transient and vile genre," which is a bit much, no doubt about it. Especially since Lugones used that phrase against Estanislao del Campo's *Fausto*, which has other, non-parodical, virtues.

F.S. When, where, and how did you meet Macedonio Fernández?

J.L.B. Macedonio Fernández was a close friend of my father's. They had proposed founding an anarchist colony in Paraguay. My father married in '98 and didn't take part in the colony. So that Macedonio Fernández belongs to my earliest memories. When we returned from Europe in 1920 or '21, Macedonio Fernández was on the dock waiting for us.

F.S. And what was he like?

J.L.B. He was a colorless man, a man of very few words, a modest man. He lived in boarding houses in the Tribunales district or in the Balvanera district—Eleventh [of September] district—where he had been born. He was a lawyer. He smoked, drank *mate*, thought, wrote with great facility and without attaching any importance to his literary work. And he was the most admirable conversationalist I've ever known.

F.S. And as a literary man, do you consider his work to be important?

J.L.B. I couldn't say. Because when I read him, I read him with Macedonio's voice, even putting on a face like Macedonio's. I don't know whether anything is there when read by people who didn't know him. For instance, Bioy Casares—who, as far as I'm concerned, is one of the best writers in Argentina— told me he had never found anything good in Macedonio. But it's because he hadn't been acquainted with him; if he had known him, he would have understood him. Macedonio had the bad habit of inventing useless neologisms. For example, instead of saying poetry is one of the fine arts, he would say: "Poetry is fineartish." Then he used to advise us writers to sign our books: "So-and-So, Buenos Aires Artist." And nonsense like that, right? Besides, since he really believed in Buenos Aires, he thought the fact that someone was popular was proof that he was worthy, because "how could Buenos Aires be wrong?" It seems a very peculiar kind of reasoning, but he really believed in that. For instance, I told him I had seen Parravicini perform and that I thought he was very bad. Macedonio had never seen him, but the fact that he was popular was enough for him. "How could an artist who is popular not be good? How can Buenos Aires be wrong?" I even remember this remark: Macedonio said to me: "Do you see what it means for someone to know he's going to be read in Buenos Aires? Now even the Spaniards are intelligent! Look at Unamuno: his latest publications aren't bad, but why? Because he knew they were going to be read in Buenos Aires." An absurd statement; how is a person going to write better or worse because he's thinking about who's going to read him?

F.S. Now that you've mentioned Macedonio's neologisms, Xul Solar comes to mind. What was Xul Solar like?

J.L.B. Xul Solar was completely different. Xul Solar abounded in neologisms, but they were made according to a plan, with the idea of enriching the Spanish language. They weren't whimsical like Macedonio's. Xul Solar felt—correctly, I believe—that the Spanish language was too long-winded and that it should be given the brevity of English. Xul Solar was something else too; Xul Solar was a mystic, he was a visionary, he was a painter. He was nothing like Macedonio. When they had to interact on occasion, they didn't get along very well. Besides, Xul Solar read widely; he was quite interested in philology. And Macedonio Fernández believed, on the contrary, in the virtues of solitary meditation. All you had to do was to tell Macedonio that someone from another country or from another era had said something and he would reject it. Once I told him that I was interested in Scandinavian mythology, and he said to me: "Scandinavian mythology is probably . . . like the mythology of the tenement house across the way." He was very fond, and so am I, of Estanislao del Campo's *Fausto*. But the reason he'd give is that it's a work that many women know by heart. He put a lot of stock in the opinion of the ladies. On the other hand, when someone spoke to him about *Martín Fierro*, he said: "Get away with that rancorous Calabrian."[22] But that was at a time when *Martín Fierro* was seen as so much swashbuckling and *Fausto* was felt to be a good-natured and very often compassionate joke. But I want to make it clear that they didn't get along together; they had nothing to do with one another. Their paths might have crossed on occasion but they didn't go out of their way to see each other. I think each one saw the other as wrong-headed, possibly as a madman.

F.S. Do you have any idea—I don't know if you've read it—that in Marechal's novel *Adán Buenosayres* . . . ?

J.L.B. No, I haven't read it because I heard that I was mentioned in it. And since I don't read anything written about me . . . I told Alicia Jurado (I'm a good friend of hers): "Look here, I'm not going to read your latest book because it's about me, and since that subject doesn't interest me, I'd rather read something else, anything else."

F.S. Yes, but in that book you're just another character, and under another name.[23]

J.L.B. Yes, but I found out I was in it, so I decided to avoid it.

F.S. I asked you that question because I wanted to know what effect it had on you—you, who have created so many fictional beings—to have yourself been turned into a character in a novel.

J.L.B. I don't know, because I haven't read the book. Besides, Marechal became a Nationalist, and that separated us. I believe he later became a Peronist too. I believe the last time I saw him was in Victoria Ocampo's home, and as he was on his way out, he told me: "You know, Borges, I've never been interested in what you've written?" I said to him: "Well, I don't find my writing interesting either; I write what I can, that's all. On the other hand, there are many lines of yours that I like. So we agree. You might possibly tell me that your writings are bad, because writers almost always think that way." I believe that was the last time I spoke with him.

F.S. How long ago was that?

J.L.B. I don't remember the date.

F.S. Weren't you both on a first-name basis, having met one another while you were both so young?

J.L.B. It's possible.

F.S. And afterward you called each other "Mister."

J.L.B. No, no; we might have called each other by our first names on that occasion too. I don't remember. The man who can tell you more about Marechal is Bernárdez, who was a friend of his. Or Norah Lange. But as for myself, I can't give you any information on Marechal. Certainly he's written some very nice poetry, naturally:

Don't deny your father, Leopoldo Marechal . . .

And the poems about the bronco buster;[24] they're very nice, too.

F.S. What has Argentinean literature lost with the death of Leopoldo Marechal?

J.L.B. Well, if you ask me that, it must be because you feel Leopoldo Marechal's work is not enough.

F.S. No. I'm saying it only in the sense that in order to write, one has to be alive.

J.L.B. I think Marechal was a good poet. I'm not familiar with his prose works. I think that within the framework of that rhetoric he used, he was an excellent poet. Or rather, an extremely skillful poet.

F.S. With a great mastery of technique.

J.L.B. Yes, and by that I don't mean to take away from his merits. It's one type of poetry; the same could be said of a good part of the work of Lugones and of Rubén Darío too, that their virtues are technical more than anything else. Now, Marechal and I hardly knew one another personally. I believe I was in his home in Villa Crespo once, and after that . . . I remember that Alfonso Reyes had founded a magazine called *Libra*,[25] and invited me to contribute to the magazine. But since there were a good number of Nationalists who contributed to that magazine, and I know people like to generalize, I wrote a letter to Reyes telling him I felt highly honored by his invitation, but that I couldn't accept it because if I were to be a contributor along with a group of young Argentinean writers who were Nationalists, people would naturally see me as a Nationalist too. And since I'm not a Nationalist, nor do I want to be taken for one, I told Reyes I'd rather not contribute to *Libra* magazine. And he answered—I don't know whether I still have the letter around somewhere—telling me it was a pity I felt that way, but that he understood my reasoning and reminding me that he was expecting me for dinner the following Sunday. Perhaps I did the wrong thing, but since at that time I was quite less well known than now, I knew that if my name were seen beside Marechal's[26] or Bernárdez' name—Bernárdez was a Nationalist too in those days—people were going to put us in *le même panier*, as the French say.

F.S. What memories do you have of Güiraldes?

J.L.B. Güiraldes had a very curious career. People looked on him as a disciple of Lugones because of *El cencerro de cristal* (The Crystal Cowbell), in which the influence of the *Lunario* is evident. Later he published *Don Segundo Sombra*; he was invested with a sudden glory. And immediately afterward, as a sort of dramatic contrast, a rough one at that, the trip to Paris and cancer and death. *Don Segundo Sombra* was done as a kind of elegy to the life of the gaucho, a way of life that had vanished. Enrique Amorim wrote *El paisano Aguilar* (Ranch Hand Aguilar); Enrique Amorim had grown up on the border between Uruguay and Brazil, grown up among gauchos and, like everyone who has been raised among gauchos, didn't have any romantic ideas about the gaucho. On the other hand, Güiraldes based his writing on childhood memories, on nostalgia for his childhood, thinking about the fact that this kind of life had disappeared. But there's a geographical circumstance too. Güiraldes wrote in the North of Buenos Aires Province, in an area already invaded—maybe that's the wrong word—by the Italian and Spanish truck farms, and in which cattle raising was disappearing. On the other hand, Amorim was raised in northern Uruguay, in a purely cattle-raising region. And, talking about that, an anecdote comes to mind: I was with Amorim in a town near the Brazilian border, and there were some horse races being held, and I saw some three hundred cowboys! And with a thoroughly Buenos Aires candor, with a thoroughly Buenos Aires ingenuousness, I said to Amorim: "Oh, wow! Three hundred gauchos!" Then he gave me a slow, sarcastic look, because he had grown up in Tangarupá, among gauchos. "Well now," he said, "seeing three hundred gauchos here is like seeing three hundred Gath & Chaves [a huge department store, similar to Macy's] employees in Buenos Aires." It's the kind of crack

Güiraldes would never have made, because he had a romantic idea of the gaucho. He saw the gaucho as something lost forever, with the preciousness of everything that's lost and with the patina of time, besides. You see, in *Don Segundo Sombra* we know almost nothing about Don Segundo. We don't know anything because Güiraldes didn't know anything about him either. He's a personage who seems to be respected by everyone else, and we don't know whether he actually is the character the boy believes him to be, or whether he's an impostor who's pulling the wool over the eyes of the boy who's telling the story.

F.S. Let's move on to the question of our national language. In 1928 you published *El idioma de los argentinos* (The Language of the Argentineans), right?

J.L.B. Yes, but it was a mistake. I believe we [the Hispanic peoples] must now accentuate our affinities and not our differences. I believe, for instance, that the Argentine Academy [of the Spanish Language] is making a mistake in collecting regionalisms. I think that what is important is to *forget* about regionalisms and to remember that we're fortunate in sharing one of the most widely disseminated languages in the world. And it's unfortunate that there exist Catamarca-isms, Buenos Aires-isms, Andalusianisms, Catalanisms. And I recall quite a good anecdote of [Roberto] Arlt's—I was somewhat acquainted with him, not very much. The González Tuñón brothers were accusing Arlt of not knowing Lunfardo [a kind of underworld slang popularized by tango lyrics]. And so Arlt answered—it's the only joke I've ever heard out of Arlt; of course, I haven't spoken with him very much—"Well," he said, "I've been raised among poor folk, in Villa Luro, among some pretty tough characters [who would be expected to employ Lunfardo], and I've never really had the time to study those things," as if to indicate that Lunfardo was something invented by the writers of those short farces that satirize local customs, or by the people who write tango lyrics. "I've been raised among some pretty tough characters and I've never really had the time to study those things." And I myself have had some acquaintance with those people too, and I've observed—anyone can observe this—that they hardly ever use Lunfardo. Or, I don't know, they might use a word of it from time to time. For example:

Era un mosaico diquero, que yugaba de quemera.[27]

The chick thought she was real cool,
Though she earned her bread at the City Dump . . .

If someone were actually to speak this way, we would think he'd gone mad, or that he's doing it for humorous effect. Because no one speaks like that. All that kind of language found in tango lyrics that Américo Castro took seriously is nothing more than a literary game.

F.S. Now that you've mentioned Américo Castro, the fact that you wrote an article called "El arte de injuriar" (The Art of Insult) comes to mind. Later, it seems, you turned theory into practice in "Las alarmas del doctor Américo Castro" (Dr. Américo Castro is Alarmed).

J.L.B. That's true. But later I met Américo Castro at Princeton. He came up to me, we each insisted that the other was right, and I said to him: "You were right; your arguments were faulty but prophetic. That cult of criminality, of vulgarity, all that culminated afterward in Peronism. You sensed it then, when we didn't sense it and were even accomplices in all that. Your arguments were, of course, faulty, because in order to study the speech habits of a country, it's better to observe how people, not the characters in a satirical farce (which is a comic genre, a parodical genre), speak. But you were right. There has arisen in my country a cult of the plebeian, and of a phony plebeian to boot, completely removed from reality." And Sarmiento had already pointed out that the speech of gaucho-style literature was much more barbaric than that of the gauchos themselves. But those authors used that brand of language because they were writing for cultivated readers for whom the fact that a person might speak that way seemed humorous. Sarmiento had already pointed that out: he pointed out the fact that the language of the gauchos—and he knew them; how could he *not* have known them?—was much more cultivated than the language of Ascasubi or of Hernández or the others; they exaggerated the barbarisms.

F.S. I understand that in your readings you've had one favorite author after another since you were young.

J.L.B. Yes, but I believe they're the same ones. It's just that I thought it was more honorable to name others. But I think they were Wells and Stevenson and Kipling from the first . . .

F.S. And no Spaniards?[28]

J.L.B. Spaniards? Well . . . *Don Quixote*, yes. And Fray Luis de León too. Spanish literature began admirably: the Spanish *romances* are beautiful. But what happened afterward? I think the decadence of Spanish literature ran parallel with the decadence of the Spanish Empire: from the time the "Invincible" Armada was destroyed, from the time Spain failed to understand Protestantism, from the time Spain remained more distant from France than we in Latin America did, from the time Spanish-American Modernism[29] was being forged in the shadow of Hugo and Verlaine while in Spain they were unaware of this.

F.S. According to what you've just said, would Quevedo and Góngora fall within the early stages of Spanish decadence?

J.L.B. There's no doubt about it. They already had a kind of rigidity, of stiffness in them which one doesn't find, for example, in Fray Luis de León. When you read Fray Luis, you realize that he was a better person than Quevedo or than Góngora, who were vain, baroque people who wanted to dazzle the reader. And they were a little younger, compared with Fray Luis. But look at the "Coplas" of Manrique, for example. Truly a great poem! And it wasn't written for the purpose of dazzling anyone. Why do I consider Fray Luis de León a better poet than Quevedo? Not line for line; Quevedo, no doubt, is more inventive verbally. But at the same time, one feels that Fray Luis de León was a better person than Quevedo. Quevedo, if he had lived at the present time, what would he have been? He would have been a follower of Franco, of course. He would have been a Nationalist. In Buenos Aires he would have been a Peronist. He was a man who didn't understand anything of what was taking place in his own time. For instance, he was unaware of the Protestant Movement, which was important. They weren't even aware of the discovery of America. They were all more interested in the disastrous wars and defeats they were suffering in Flanders than in the New World. And Montesquieu realized this. He said: "The Indies [i. e. America] are the main thing; Spain is secondary: *L'Espagne n'est que l'accessoire*." And there was no Spaniard who understood that, not even Cervantes, I believe. Cervantes was more interested in the wars in Flanders, which, of course, were disastrous, because they were beaten by people who weren't even soldiers.

F.S. What do you think of medieval Spanish literature? The *Poema del Cid* or the Archpriest of Hita, for example?

J.L.B. I think the *Cid* is a dull and unimaginative poem. Think of the heroic spirit there is in the [French] *Chanson de Roland*, centuries earlier. Think of Anglo-Saxon epic poetry and of Scandinavian poetry. The *Cid* actually is a very slow poem, very clumsily done.

F.S. And the Archpriest of Hita?

J.L.B. I don't think he's a very important author. Now, Saint John of the Cross was; he was a great poet, of course. And Garcilaso, too. But what was Garcilaso? He was an Italian poet gone astray in Spain. This is so true that his contemporaries didn't understand him. Castillejo, for example, never came to have a feel—as Lugones remembers and Jaimes Freyre remembered too—for the music of the hendecasyllable. They were accustomed to the octosyllable, just like our gaucho troubadours. And then there's Spain's eighteenth century: it's impoverished to the utmost. The nineteenth century is a disgrace! Spain has no novelist like the Portuguese Eça de Queiroz, for example. And at present all the important poets that Spain has produced are the products of Modernism, and Modernism came to them from Spanish-America. And Spanish-language prose has been renovated by Groussac and by Reyes [writing in the Americas].

F.S. Did you know Groussac personally?

J.L.B. No, I never had the courage to meet him because I knew that what I was writing was very bad, and I also knew he was an extremely severe man. I can tell you an anecdote about Groussac. He was being interviewed. First they asked him what he was doing. He said: "What can I do in a country in which Lugones is [considered] a Hellenist?" They spoke to him about *Don Segundo Sombra*. He said: "A wild and wooly book written by a socialite, but he'll have to do some stretching"—republishing a certain joke on Hernández, no doubt, or on Estanislao del Campo—"he'll have to stretch his poncho so no one will see his frock coat underneath." And I say "republishing" a joke because the frock coat was no longer being worn in 1926. Then they asked him about Ricardo Rojas: "A horticulturalist," he said, referring to flowery style, etc. He had the deepest contempt for him. He had a low opinion of all the gaucho-style writers. He used to refer to Estanislao del Campo as a "law-office gaucho troubadour." (Groussac tells of his having been in Victor Hugo's house, of his having tried to generate some excitement in himself by thinking: "Here I am in Hugo's house; this all is a part of his life, of his memory . . . Nevertheless," he says, "I felt as unemotional as though I were in the home of José Hernández, the author of *Martín Fierro*.") And they went on that way; they would mention authors, and he would make short work of them all. Finally they spoke to him about a writer whom I don't admire and whom he did— but he was a personal friend of his: Enrique Larreta. Then he pretended to be somewhat surprised and said: "Ah! Then are we going to discuss literature too today?", as though none of the others had any literary merit.

F.S. You're saying that Groussac was ill-tempered.

J.L.B. It seems that way. He died in the room next door. Because his bedroom was here [in the National Library]. The family lived upstairs.

second
conversation

Borges' Paradise — Johannes Brahms Helps Dr. H. Bustos Domecq — Stupid Sports — Rough Drafts — Untranslatable Shakespeare — Gossip in José Mármol — Importance of Eça de Queiroz — Enrique Banchs, Ant Exterminator — The *Martín Fierro* Epitaphs — Andrés Selpa's Felicitous Error — The Fantasy of Fernando Quiñones

F.S. If you had to define what literature has meant in your life, what would you say?

J.L.B. Before I ever wrote a single line, I knew, in some mysterious and therefore unequivocal way, that I was destined for literature. What I didn't realize at first is that besides being destined to be a reader, I was also destined to be a writer, and I don't think one is less important than the other. I remember a poem of mine, the "Poema de los dones" (Poem of Gifts), which I wrote when I was appointed Director of the National Library in the year of the Liberating Revolution. I discovered that I was surrounded by seven hundred thousand books and that I could no longer read them. In that poem I compare my fate to that of Groussac, and I say:

> I, who pictured Paradise
> in the form of a library.

The way others have pictured Paradise as a garden, for example. For me, the idea of being surrounded with books has always been a beautiful idea. Even now that I can't read books, their mere proximity fills me with a sort of happiness; at times, a somewhat nostalgic happiness, but happiness still and all.

F.S. When you began to lose your vision, what did you find in music?

J.L.B. I'm very ignorant about music. If you speak to me about music, I tend to think about the blues, about spirituals, about milongas,[1] about tangos before the time of . . . What's the name of that famous singer?

F.S. Gardel.

J.L.B. Yes, the tangos before the time of Gardel. Let me tell you this anecdote. I was working—and I still am—in collaboration with Adolfo Bioy Casares. While we were working, Silvina Ocampo, Bioy's wife, would put records on. After a while we found that there were certain records that left us cold or annoyed us, and those were recordings of Debussy or of Wagner. On the other hand, there were others which infused us with a kind of fervor, which helped us to work, and we ascertained that those recordings were of Brahms. And I think my musical biography begins and ends here. At the same time, I've felt Pater's statement to be possibly true, that all the arts aspire to the condition of music. Possibly, because in music, form and content are one; we can't separate them. On the other hand, a novel, for instance, can be read and can be related afterward, and I don't think one melody is translatable into another, although a musician doubtless can analyze it. It happens that I've always had great respect for music, so much so that although I've composed milonga lyrics, I've always thought it absurd for words to be added to music because I think music is a language, perhaps not a more precise one, but a much more effective language than *language*, than words. I suppose all musicians feel the same way. Besides, I think poetry has its own music. For instance, when I was told that certain compositions of Verlaine had been set to music, it occurred to me that Verlaine would have been indignant about this, because the music was already in the words. Now, as for the fact that I've lost my sight, the process has been so gradual that it was never a sudden blow. I mean to say, the world has been becoming more and more blurred for me; books have lost their letters, my friends have lost their faces, but all that has been happening over a period of many years. Besides, I knew that would be my fate because my father, my grandmother, that is, my grandparents, and, I think, my great-great-grandfather, were blind when they died. My vision was never good. Proof of that is that if I think about my childhood I don't think of the neighborhood, I don't think about my parents' faces. What I think about are miniscule things, seen close up. For example, I think I remember more or less the illustrations in encyclopedias, in travel books, in *The Thousand and One Nights*, in dictionaries. I think I remember quite precisely the stamps in a large album there was at home, and all that because they were the only things I saw well, which is typical of the minute vision of the nearsighted.

F.S. Since you've referred to that period of your childhood, I'd like to ask you if you took part in the usual leisure activities of the time and, if so, what they were. I don't know . . . maybe soccer?

J.L.B. Soccer, at that time, was relegated to one or two English schools, but I suppose most people probably hadn't heard of it or weren't interested in it.[2] At any rate, it was probably thought of as the sport of some rich kids in the schools of Lomas or Belgrano. And I think it's strange—coincidentally, I was talking about this last night—it's strange that England—which I love so much—provokes so much hatred in the world but that nevertheless one argument that could be used is never used against England: that of having filled the world with stupid sports. It's strange that people who don't like England don't confront her with having filled the world with cricket, with golf—although golf is Scottish—with soccer. I think that is one of the sins which could be imputed to England. It's true that I believe she has also produced a few card games that perhaps require intelligence: whist or bridge. But I don't believe them to be comparable to chess, for example. But there are other sports that I've engaged in, without calling them sports, of course. As a child I was a fair horseman, as every Argentinean has been. Spills figure in my biography, as in the biography of every Argentinean. And I've been a good swimmer and a tireless walker. You see I've listed physical exercise which doesn't necessarily lend itself to competition. What I find especially bad in sports is the idea that someone has to win and someone has to lose, and that this fact gives rise to rivalries. I even suspect that most of the people who say they're interested in soccer aren't interested at all since if they were, they wouldn't care who wins or who loses. I think that's what happens in chess. There are certain chess matches which are famous, and it doesn't matter much who finally won. On the other hand, I've met people who tell me: "I like soccer." But it turns out they don't; what they want is for such and such a team to win, which I feel is totally alien to the idea of the game *per se*. I happened to notice this during a well-known match between Uruguayans and Argentineans: the spectators were already for one side or the other even before the game started. This seemed really strange to me since how could they know before the game started who were going to play better or worse, who were going to be stronger or more skillful? But all this, of course, is promoted commercially. At one time it might have involved rivalry among different neighborhoods; at present, I think not, because the players don't even come from the neighborhoods of each team, but are bought and sold. It's totally a matter of chance. For example, I don't believe that all the players on the Chacarita Juniors were born in Chacarita.

F.S. Worse than that, the entire Chacarita club has moved to San Martín.

J.L.B. You see? And I suppose it must be the same with any other team.

F.S. Did you used to like those comical movies of Chaplin or of Laurel and Hardy?

J.L.B. Laurel and Hardy's came much later. Among those of Chaplin, I still like the earlier ones better than the more ambitious ones he made afterward. For instance, I think *A King in New York* is pretty bad. I think the film he made against Hitler[3] is bad too.

F.S. I've been speaking with Raúl González Tuñón for several days now, and because he has a profound admiration for your first three books of poetry, he deplores your having abandoned the themes and the style of those poems. Supposing Raúl were a prosecuting attorney and that you had to justify yourself, how would you answer him?

J.L.B. I believe it's a false accusation. As for the style, I've modified it by purifying it in order to make it more direct and simpler. At that time I still believed a little in Ultraism, in Lugones' idea that new metaphors had to be invented. On the other hand, I now try to write plainly. As for the themes, I think I haven't changed. In any case, re-reading my first books of poetry, I see there are many poems that must be the rough drafts of those I wrote afterward. For example, the different poems I've dedicated to my great-grandfather, Colonel Suárez. In the first book there are eight or nine lines on this subject.[4] Then, in a later book, we find "Página para recordar al coronel Suárez, vencedor en Junín"[5] (A Page to Commemorate Colonel Suárez, Victor at Junín), with which I think I've exhausted the subject. I also wrote a poem to my grandfather Borges—it's in my first book and is very poorly done;[6] later I did it somewhat better[7] and now I'm going to do it in prose and I believe I'll do a better job of it. The themes of philosophical perplexity, the idea of time, the idea of the oneiric character of the world are already in *Fervor de Buenos Aires* (A Passion for Buenos Aires) and are also in *Elogio de la sombra* (In Praise of Darkness), for example. So that I believe I have no need to defend myself from an accusation which has no basis in truth. That is, I have no reason to justify something that hasn't happened. Besides, Di Giovanni[8] has found affinities between old texts of mine and more recent ones. Some days ago we were re-reading a story[9] in which there is an enumeration of what someone sees in a magic mirror he has formed with the ink-filled palm of his hand. And Di Giovanni told me: "Here is the rough draft of the story 'El Aleph.'" And it's true: in those six or seven lines is the rough draft of the story I would later write. When I was in Texas, a tall blonde girl said to me: "When you wrote the poem 'El Gólem' (The Golem), did you propose to utilize the same plot as that of 'Las ruinas circulares' (The Circular Ruins)?" And I told her: "I didn't propose to, but I'm greatly indebted to you for pointing out that affinity—which is a real one—to me, and now there is the almost magic fact that I've traveled to the end of the world, from Buenos Aires to Texas, to the edge of the desert, and you reveal something to me about my own work of which I was unaware."

F.S. Raúl González Tuñón showed me a copy of the first edition of *Luna de enfrente* (Moon Across the Way), which you dedicated to him with these words: "To the other poet of the outskirts, Raúl González Tuñón." Did Raúl and you used to consider yourselves the only two poets of the outskirts?

J.L.B. No, we didn't consider ourselves the only ones. We shared a predilection for writing about the outlying slums. I couldn't find a better term than *of the outskirts*, because *of the outlying slums* would be a bit derogatory, wouldn't it? And I couldn't put "To the other poet of Buenos Aires," because the poet of Buenos Aires was Fernández Moreno.

F.S. Do you like the poems of González Tuñón?

J.L.B. I really don't remember them very well right now. He had written a few nice poems on the Spanish Civil War,[10] and I think he handled Spanish themes better than Argentinean ones, don't you? And it's only natural because he's the son of Spaniards and had a much greater feel for Spanish rather than for Argentinean themes.

F.S. You, who are so fond of stories about toughs and hoodlums, what do you think of *Un guapo del 900* (A Turn-of-the-Century Hoodlum), by Eichelbaum?

J.L.B. Now I remember it with some confusion, but I remember that when I saw that play in the theater I liked it. But I wouldn't be able to tell you the plot. I do remember that I liked the character. I met Eichelbaum, I think through Mastronardi, because they're both from Entre Ríos Province. Eichelbaum must have been born in one of the Jewish colonies founded by Theodore Hirsch,[11] but I'm not sure.

F.S. That was Gerchunoff's territory, wasn't it?

J.L.B. Probably, although Gerchunoff actually was born in Odessa. But it's the same ambience as Eichelbaum's. Now you see, that book of Gerchunoff's, *Los gauchos judíos* (*The Jewish Gauchos*), has a title that doesn't agree with the text. Because when you read the book, you realize that those Jewish immigrants weren't gauchos; they were farmers. You can even see that in the chapter headings themselves: "Plowing," "Threshing," etc. That doesn't have anything to do with the gaucho, who was a horseman and not a farmer.[12]

F.S. What role do the works of Shakespeare play in your life?

J.L.B. They play an important role, but outside of *Macbeth* and *Hamlet*, they pertain to verbal memories rather than to memories of situations or of characters. For example, what I've re-read most in Shakespeare are the sonnets. I could quote so many lines for you . . . Just as I could quote so many lines from his dramatic works too . . . I think of Shakespeare above all as a craftsman of words. For example, I see him closer to Joyce than to the great novelists, where character is the most important thing. That's the reason I'm skeptical about translations of Shakespeare, because since what is most essential and most precious in him is the verbal aspect, I wonder to what extent the verbal can be translated. A short time ago someone told me: "It's impossible to translate Shakespeare into Spanish." And I answered him: "As impossible as it is to translate him into English." Because if we were to translate Shakespeare into an English which is not the English of Shakespeare, a great deal would be lost. There are even sentences of Shakespeare's that only exist if pronounced with those same words, in that same order and with that same melody.

F.S. But what you've just said is, in a way, a slur against Shakespeare, if we remember that you once praised those books which, like *Don Quixote*, can come away from the worst translations unscathed.[13]

J.L.B. Yes, the truth is that I'm contradicting myself here. Because by the way, I remember that we saw, together with Letizia Álvarez de Toledo, a production of *Macbeth* in Spanish, performed by terrible actors, with terrible stage sets, using an abominable translation, and yet we left the theater very, very thrilled. So I believe I made a slip when I said what I did before. And I don't mind your recording my retraction, because I don't think of myself as infallible, not at all, not even when it comes to my own work.

F.S. Readers usually believe, unjustly perhaps, that they can demand a particular kind of behavior from a writer they admire. I, who have been dazzled by the stories in *Ficciones* (Fictions) and in *El Aleph* (The Aleph), take the liberty of criticizing you for having given up, in the stories of *El informe de Brodie* (Brodie's Report), those complex plots. How would you answer me?

J.L.B. My answer to you is that I've done it deliberately, because since I've been told there are other people who are writing that type of literature, and no doubt they're doing it better than I, I've attempted something different. But it's possible that this is my conscious motive and, for that very reason, not too important. Instead, I believe there is something that has led me to write stories of another type: being tired of mirrors, of labyrinths, of people who are other people, of games with time. Why not suppose that being tired of all that, I want to write stories somewhat the way others do?

F.S. Of course, I understand that. But, speaking for myself, I wouldn't think of reading *El informe de Brodie*[14] again, yet I read and re-read *El Aleph* (I know it almost by heart).

J.L.B. That might be due to the fact that when I wrote *El Aleph*, the writing was carried out in a kind of literary plenitude. On the other hand, it could be that I'm now in a state of decline and my current works could reflect a sort of decadence in me. It would be perfectly natural because it's biologically understandable. In August I'll be seventy-two years old, and it's only logical for what I'm writing now to be inferior to what I wrote earlier. I think this biological explanation is a pretty likely one. But, at the same time, since I'm in the habit of writing, I keep doing what I can. Now, I don't know if you've read a story of mine called "El congreso" (The Congress),[15] because I got the idea for that story more than thirty years ago but wrote it a short time ago. There might possibly be some disparity in the plot, which of course is a fantastic plot—not fantastic in the supernatural sense but rather in the sense of impossible—because it has to do with a mystical experience that I haven't had. My aim was to narrate something in which I didn't fully believe to see how it would turn out.

F.S. Putting aside any sympathies these two writers' opposition to Rosas might awaken in you, do you find any literary value in the works of Echeverría and of Mármol?

J.L.B. Yes, Echeverría was (aside, perhaps, from the English travelers) the first one to see the literary possibilities of the plains, of the Indian raids, of the women captives. And I think the story "El matadero" is a very good story. As good as the poem "La refalosa" by Ascasubi, which it greatly resembles, incidentally. Now, in Mármol's case, although he could be easily censured page for page, and even more so, line by line, he is nevertheless the one who is responsible for the image we all have of the Rosas era. Furthermore, he has preserved an enormous quantity of details and gossip of the era with which, thanks to him, we're now familiar. I'm going to give you an example which isn't very important. If it hadn't been for Mármol's *Amalia*, who would now know that the poet Juan Crisóstomo Lafinur was a steady client at the brothels?[16] No one. They're insignificant facts, but history is made of those *petites histoires*. I think that, in general, when we say "in Rosas' time," without realizing it we're citing Mármol. And I think the very same people who are opposed to him picture the times of Rosas according to Mármol and not according to better books, as for example, *Rosas y su tiempo* (Rosas and his Time), by Ramos Mejía, which provides a more accurate picture of what Rosas' times were like.

F.S. What do you think about the works of Eça de Queiroz?

J.L.B. Eça de Queiroz was one of the best novelists of the nineteenth century. I remember that my father brought my mother a Spanish version of *The Illustrious House of Ramires* [*A ilustre casa de Ramires*]. My mother had never heard anyone speak of Eça de Queiroz (and she's not particularly interested in literature anyway). She read the book and said to my father: "It's one of the best novels I've ever read in my life." Afterward, I read his novels in Portuguese and came to that same conclusion. And I don't think it's necessary to compare him with other writers of the Iberian Peninsula, because in that way we would give Eça de Queiroz too easy a victory if we say he's better than Galdós, or than Pereda, or than Valera. No: he's a great writer. There probably are novelists as good as he in the nineteenth century, but there are none superior.

F.S. And if we were to compare him, although one is very different from the other, with Dickens and with Flaubert?

J.L.B. Dickens has created a kind of world of his own, and Eça de Queiroz did not do that. A fantastic world—shall we say—or rather, a grotesque world. In Flaubert's case, the influence on Eça de Queiroz is evident. And I believe that *Cousin Bazilio [O primo Bazilio]* is quite superior to *Madame Bovary* although evidently it is based on *Madame Bovary*.

F.S. Maybe the fact that he was born in Portugal impeded his becoming famous.

J.L.B. Yes, of course, it's quite possible that he's been handicapped by the fact that he was Portuguese.

F.S. Yes, because had he been French or English, he'd be very famous.

J.L.B. He would be much better known if he had been Spanish. Besides, you see, he's written disparate works. For example, *The Mandarin [O mandarim]* is a splendid story of the fantastic, and at the same time is humorous. And this story has very little to do with *The City and the Mountains [A cidade e as serras]*, with *Cousin Bazilio*, with *The Maias [Os Maia]*, with *Father Amaro's Crime [O crime do padre Amaro]* . . . And in *The Illustrious House of Ramires* there is a great character, one who's a little ridiculous but very lovable, a congenial fellow. But now it seems there's a tendency to rehabilitate him, because in a literary supplement of *The Times*, Eça de Queiroz is spoken of as one of the greatest novelists of the nineteenth century.

F.S. I don't think they've discovered anything new.

J.L.B. That's true, but as they say, better late than never. It's better that they've come to that conclusion now than for them never to have done so. His own fellow countrymen may possibly have thought little of him. Maybe they saw him as an ironic Frenchman. I think it's quite probable. Because since everyone feels that what's typically Portuguese is nostalgia, *saudade*, a certain melancholy . . . And you find these things in Eça de Queiroz, but you find hundreds of other things too. So it's probable that his fellow Portuguese saw him as being outside the Portuguese tradition. And this is true, since he wrote pretty much within the tradition of certain French authors, especially in the tradition of Flaubert and Daudet. But that's of no interest to us: the fact is that Eça de Queiroz is a great writer. There's no doubt at all about this.

F.S. Is it true that when you were asked about Jorge Isaacs, while you were in Colombia, you ironically asked who Jorge Isaacs was?

J.L.B. Was that said here in Argentina?

F.S. I've never seen it in writing, but I've heard it said.

J.L.B. No. I never said that. Why, I read *María* as a boy and I remember the book rather well. Besides, I would never have been that impolite. It's an apocryphal anecdote. First of all, I've read *María*—without any excess of admiration—but I remember it quite well. In the second place, I would never have answered in such an impertinent manner.

F.S. If you had to write a history of Argentine literature which, because of editorial requirements, could contain only five authors, which ones would you choose?

J.L.B. Goodness, what a difficult question . . . ! Well, let's see . . . In the first place, Sarmiento; then, Ascasubi; then, Hernández; then, Lugones, and then . . . We're getting very close to our own era and I'm going to step on some contemporary's toes . . . But, let's say . . . It might be Almafuerte or it might possibly be Martínez Estrada.

F.S. Or Banchs, perhaps . . .

J.L.B. Or Banchs, perhaps. Although, when you think about it, Banchs is the author of only one important book, *La urna* (The Urn). But even so, it could be Banchs. I knew Banchs personally. I was so disillusioned conversing with him . . . It was the first time I saw him. It was at one of the literary luncheons[17] of *Nosotros* magazine. I happened to be seated next to Banchs. I told him I had a copy of *La urna* at home which he had autographed for my father and I told him I knew many of the sonnets by heart. Then, to chastise me, Banchs spoke to me the whole time about the ravages of ants and of the advantages and disadvantages of cyanide, and this lasted through the entire luncheon and I didn't know how to escape from that immense ant hill. And he kept speaking ever so slowly and so precisely about ants . . . Later I learned that I shouldn't have spoken to him about his writing. Then I ran into him again, and Banchs spoke to me about the young American poets, who he said interested him a great deal. Then I tried to follow the conversation. But, as he didn't know any English and had read who knows what translation of them and didn't even link them to their ambience, I suspect he didn't have any great interest in those poets. I think what he was afraid of was that someone might talk about his writing. I know of individuals from different publishing houses who went to see him to propose an edition of his complete works, telling him, furthermore, that if he liked, he could add a prologue in which he could say he completely dissociated himself from the contents of the book, that he had written those poems on various dates, that he was no longer the same person he used to be, etc. And he refused. And the reason Banchs gave was this: "People think I'm a good poet, but if they were to re-read what I've written, they would realize that I'm very mediocre." Naturally, I don't believe that was the real reason. Banchs was a very peculiar person, anyway. He was a member of the Argentine Academy of Literature and knew the Academy's regulations by heart. He'd say, for instance: "Clause A of article 27 says such-and-such, which rules out what you want to do." So that it was very hard to argue with him. Because if he took the Academy's regulations as a kind of sacred text and quoted those lines as if they were verses of the Holy Spirit, a person didn't know how to answer him. Now, how he took the trouble to learn the regulations by heart is something I can't figure out. You must be aware of what the statutes of the Academy can be like. Everyone knows they can't be overly strict, that they have to be somewhat flexible and that if you disobey them, you're not going to go to jail over it, nor are you going to suffer from feelings of guilt for the rest of your life.

F.S. The other day I was re-reading a journal in which some of the famous epitaphs of the "Graveyard" in *Martín Fierro* were reproduced.[18] Do you know who wrote them?

J.L.B. No, I don't know. I never wrote any and had nothing to do with them. Besides, I had very little to do with the *Martín Fierro* group;[19] instead I belonged to the *Proa* group, a review we put out with Brandán Caraffa, Rojas Paz, and Güiraldes. I don't know who the authors of the epitaphs were. Possibly Ernesto Palacio used to write them. Yes, I believe it was Ernesto who wrote them. But I'm not sure. There could very well have been several authors. I wonder who they were.

F.S. Might not Nalé Roxlo have been one of them? He has the right wit for that sort of thing . . .

J.L.B. No, I don't think Nalé . . . Because he didn't belong to that group. We considered him—entirely without cause—a very old-fashioned poet, a kind of vague disciple of Lugones—of Lugones at his least interesting. I don't think it was Nalé. Who could have written that? Ernesto Palacio . . . maybe Alfonso de Laferrère . . . , maybe Rega Molina wrote one or more too . . . It wasn't Bernárdez; it wasn't Molinari; nor was it I . . . Those epitaphs were very well versified too.

F.S. There was a very funny one dedicated to Jorge Max Rohde . . .

J.L.B. Oh, yes, the one about Jorge Max Rohde was done by Nalé Roxlo. Because I remember a conversation on this matter.

F.S. I don't know if I'm right, but I have the impression that you probably don't like Rabelais.

J.L.B. Yes, he's the most boring author in the world. And I've tried so hard to admire him . . . And I was happy to discover that Groussac says: "Rabelais tells the same story, ruining it as he always does." I don't understand that idea of using accumulation . . . Of course, in that way he's very similar to Bustos Domecq . . . I mean . . . Bustos Domecq is very similar to him. I think what Rabelais was interested in was presenting an exhibition of synonyms. For example: "They played." And afterwards come: "chess, checkers, blackjack, bridge, poker, canasta, dice . . ."

F.S. In an article on Hawthorne,[20] you say that James Fenimore Cooper is "a sort of Eduardo Gutiérrez infinitely inferior to Eduardo Gutiérrez." Isn't that somewhat exaggerated?

J.L.B. Eduardo Gutiérrez' prose can be looked at in two ways. If you examine each one of his sentences individually, you see that they're rather pretentious and that they're too wordy. Nevertheless, if you consider his work as a whole, you believe in what he's saying. The fact is that I tried to read Fenimore Cooper and gave up, while on the other hand I've read and re-read Eduardo Gutiérrez. Of course, the fact that Gutiérrez was a friend of the family might have something to do with it . . . Besides, I think Gutiérrez was closer to what he wrote about than Fenimore Cooper was, although no doubt Fenimore Cooper must have known Indians too. Güiraldes said: "Up until now the only chance of our having a novelist in our literature was Eduardo Gutiérrez, a chance that was wasted or missed in our eternal squandering of talent." But what I don't know is whether Güiraldes said that in favor of Gutiérrez or against him.

F.S. In a not too distant era, women writers were viewed as curiosities. At present we have in our country four female writers whose names frequently appear in print: Silvina Bullrich, Marta Lynch, Silvina Ocampo, and Beatriz Guido. What is your opinion of each of them?

J.L.B. In Silvina Ocampo's case, I think her poetry is much superior to her prose. Her prose in overworked; I don't think that type of prose is right for stories. On the other hand, that style is more admissible in poetry, isn't it? With respect to the three other female writers, the truth is that I am so little acquainted with their work that I really can't say anything. Now, I think *Cuadernos de infancia* (Childhood Copybook), by Norah Lange, is a very good book. Of course it's not exactly a novel, but rather memories of the Province of Mendoza.

F.S. What do you find more difficult: writing free verse or poetry with a regular meter?

J.L.B. I find it harder to write free verse. Because if there isn't some kind of inner drive it can't be done. On the other hand, using a regular meter is a matter of patience, of application . . . Once you've written one line, you're forced to use certain rhymes, the number of rhymes is not infinite; the rhymes that can be used without incongruity are few in number . . . That is, when I have to *fabricate* something, I *fabricate* a sonnet, but I wouldn't be able to *fabricate* a poem in free verse.

F.S. How do you feel about the fact that everyone recognizes you in the street?

J.L.B. Well, I wouldn't say *everyone*, but I find it pleasant to be greeted by people I don't know. I feel friendship toward them and I feel grateful . . . Once I met a boxer, I think his name was Selpa. I was with Emma Risso Platero, we were leaving a restaurant on Esmeralda Street, and Selpa came up to me and embraced me. I felt slightly uncomfortable, but at the same time, grateful, you know? Selpa, instead of calling me *Jorge Luis Borges*, called me *José Luis Borges*, and I realized it wasn't a mistake; it was a correction. Because *Jorge Luis Borges* is very harsh; on the other hand, *José Luis Borges* sounds much softer. Why repeat a sound as ugly as *orge*? I wouldn't *urge* one to repeat *orge*, you see? I think, in the long run, I'm going to figure in the history of literature as *José Luis Borges*.

F.S. Well, as a matter of fact, you appear as *José Luis* in the *Larousse* dictionary, no doubt through a printer's error.[21]

J.L.B. That's all right: printer's errors usually tell the truth. Right now, I'd like to sign my name *Luis Borges*. But everyone tells me that would be looked on as an eccentricity; that, although *Jorge Luis Borges* is ugly, people are already accustomed to that ugliness. At any rate, it would be better to try to find a completely different pseudonym, because *Luis Borges* is somewhat removed from *Jorge Luis Borges*, but not enough so for the relationship not to be noticed.

F.S. In the book *Historias de la Argentina* by Fernando Quiñones, there are some pages devoted to a description of how a conversation with Borges was so fascinating for Quiñones that he missed the plane on which he was going to return to Spain.[22] Do you remember that conversation?

J.L.B. No. That conversation never existed and Quiñones didn't miss any plane. It's a generous invention of Quiñones'.

F.S. But are you familiar with the pages?

J.L.B. No, I'm not familiar with them, but I know the episode never took place. It must be one of Quiñones' tall stories.

F.S. Among other things, he says you told him that God's style resembles Victor Hugo's style . . .

J.L.B. Well, I probably did say that. Maybe I said it, I don't remember.

F.S. And you also told him that sometimes a poor title wasn't enough to guarantee writing a good work.

J.L.B. Well, I wish I had said that. The most I could have said is that the most famous works don't generally have good titles. Although some do. It's possible I said it, but most likely not. But, that business about Quiñones' having missed his plane must be something he made up.

F.S. The incident in those pages takes place, I believe, in the hallway of your apartment house on Maipú Street,[23] next to the elevator. Quiñones says he was about to open the elevator door and then you started to say something. And he was losing time because he was listening to what you were saying, until he finally missed his plane.

J.L.B. Well, we have Quiñones' imagination to thank for all that. At any rate, those pages belong to the literature of fantasy.

third
conversation

Gaucho Musical Comedy — Borges' Films — The Reaction of the
Masses — The Dream of Heroes — Cortázar's First Short Story —
Carlos Mastronardi — Martínez Estrada's Mistrust — Death on the
Arrow — Farce of October 17th — The Unfaithful Detective — The
Revolution of '55 — An Argument Against Democracy — Historical
Revisionism — Schopenhauer and Hitler

F.S. Did you see the film version of *Martín Fierro*?[1]

J.L.B. It would be more accurate to say I heard it because
when it comes to seeing, we're dealing with hyperbole or metaphor in my case; I see very little . . .

F.S. Well, within the limits of what you saw or heard, what
can you tell us?

J.L.B. The truth is that I didn't find the picture interesting and I have the impression that the director didn't either.
This is so much the case that I wondered why he had selected
a subject that evidently left him cold. Of course, I feel there
are various errors in the movie. First of all, I see it conceptu-
alized as a musical comedy. One keeps hearing that kind of
music that's now called *folk* or *country* music, and anyone who
has lived in the country knows that months at a time can go
by without one's hearing a single guitar. On the other hand,
in this movie one receives the almost continuous impression
of a folk festival. Besides, I think Hernández' purpose in writing the poem was to show how the War Ministry, through the
draft, through obligatory service on the frontier, ruined men;
that is, to demonstrate how Martín Fierro starts out being a
good man, a respected country man, and then how army service turns him into a deserter, a murderer, a drunkard, an out-

law, and how finally, in complete innocence, he goes over to the Indians' side. That is, he takes part in the conquest of the wilderness without understanding what it was all about. I think this might be very true to life; I think the soldiers undoubtedly understood very little about those things. They were gauchos and couldn't have had any concept of nationhood, let alone think they represented the cause of civilization against the forces of barbarism. All that could have been capitalized on in the film, yet by the end of the movie one doesn't know if Martín Fierro should be considered a poor devil who has been compelled by circumstances to be a murderer and a deserter, or if he should be regarded as an admirable character, one who is admired by the producers of the film. Furthermore, I think that if there is something obvious when reading *Martín Fierro* (and be it known that I can recite many pages by heart and that I've gotten a book[2] ready together with Adolfo Bioy Casares in which all the gaucho-style poetry from Bartolomé Hidalgo to Hernández is brought together and in which, naturally, there are works of Ascasubi, of Estanislao del Campo, of Lussich, and of others, in addition to all of *Martín Fierro*, annotated), it is that this book, in opposition to other works of the same genre, is a deliberately colorless book. For instance, Estanislao del Campo's *Fausto* was written in full color:

> On a strawberry roan,
> a new mustang, a racer

In it we have descriptions of the pampas, of the landscape. On the other hand, the film *Martín Fierro* is filled with color, as opposed to the book which is a rather colorless book, a sad book, one in which there are never any descriptions of the prairie, which is fine because a gaucho wouldn't have seen these things pictorially. In short, I felt it was a film which I don't have the nerve to call good, and I think the director would have to agree with me entirely. I think it was produced possibly as a commercial venture with no great enthusiasm for the text.

F.S. I understand that Torre Nilsson had previously filmed your short story "Emma Zunz."[3]

J.L.B. Yes, he did film it, and I really don't think he did a good job of it. He added a sentimental story that had no business being there and filled it with all kinds of sentimental details that seemed to contradict the story, which is a harsh one. I advised him that a film couldn't be made out of "Emma Zunz." The plot was too brief—I had written it hurriedly, and it would have been much better to make three short films: one with a short story by Mujica Láinez, let's say; another with a story of Silvina Ocampo's or Adolfo Bioy Casares', let's say; and then a story of mine which could have done without the insertion of totally extraneous episodes. But he said "no," that he thought a film could be made out of a story as brief as that, and he did it, but he loaded it with sentimental episodes that weaken the film.

F.S. Did you like the film version of "Hombre de la esquina rosada" (Streetcorner Man)?[4]

J.L.B. Yes, I like it so much that . . . I can now confess that I had my doubts about it, because I don't like the story, for various reasons. And yet I thought the film—despite some perhaps inevitable padding, since they too persisted in making a long film—infinitely superior to the story. I saw the film two or three times. I like it very much; I felt the actors did a good job and that the direction was excellent. So that I believe the film version improves upon the original text.

F.S. What can you tell us about the movie *Invasión*?[5]

J.L.B. There's a film I really found very interesting and I can talk about it with complete freedom since a third of the film (if these things can be measured) is mine, because I made it in collaboration with Muchnik and with Adolfo Bioy Casares. In any case, it's a fantasy film, the type of fantasy that could be characterized as new. It's not science-fiction in the style of Wells or of Bradbury. There aren't any supernatural elements either. The invaders don't come from some other world and it's

not psychological fantasy either; the characters don't behave—
as they often do in the works of Henry James or of Kafka—in
a manner contrary to ordinary human behavior. It deals with a
fantastic situation, the situation of a city (which, in spite of its
very different topography, obviously is Buenos Aires) besieged
by powerful invaders and defended—it's not known why—by a
group of civilians. Those civilians, of course, are not that latter-
day version of Douglas Fairbanks named James Bond. No, they
are men like all men; they're not especially brave nor, except
for one, exceptionally strong. They're simply people who try
to save their country from that peril and who die or get themselves killed without any particular epic bombast. But I wanted
the film essentially to be epic; that is, what the men do is epi-
cal but they are not heroes. And I believe the epic is just this,
because if the characters of the epic are endowed with exceptional strength or with magical powers, then what they do has
no great value. On the other hand, here we have a group of men,
not all of them young, some of them rather ordinary (one of
them is a family man), and these people are equal to the mis-
sion they've cut out for themselves. And I think that aside from
the unusual nature of this plot, we've successfully solved the
great technical problem we used to have (which I suppose is
the same problem faced by the directors of Westerns): the fact
that there has to be many violent deaths (previously this used
to be the case with gangster movies, which I don't know if they
make any more; I think not), the fact that there has to be many
violent deaths and that these violent deaths, nevertheless, have
to be different; they can't be repetitious and monotonous. So
that—I'll say it again—we've attempted (I don't know with
what luck) a new type of fantastic film: a film based on a situation not found in the real world, and which must nevertheless be accepted by the spectator's imagination. I believe that
in one of Coleridge's books that theme is taken up, the theme
dealing with what the spectator in a theater believes or what
the reader of a book believes. The spectator is conscious of the

fact that he's in a theater; the reader knows he's reading a piece of fiction. And yet he must believe in some way in what he's reading. Coleridge found the *mot juste*. He spoke of "a willing suspension of disbelief."[6] I hope we've achieved that during the two hours of *Invasión*. I also want to remind you that Troilo has composed, for a milonga the lyrics of which are entirely mine, some admirable music. Furthermore, I believe motion pictures, like other genres (theater, lecture), are always a work of collaboration. That is, I think the success of a film, of a lecture, of a play, depends on the public as well. And I was curious to learn how Buenos Aires would receive that film, which doesn't resemble any other film and doesn't seek to resemble any other film. In any event, we've launched a new genre—I think—in the history of motion pictures.

F.S. Do you care about the opinion of readers or spectators?

J.L.B. They're not exactly the same thing. It's possible that a book won't attract any attention when it's published; it may be discovered afterward. On the other hand, in the case of a film (and this makes everything more dramatic; the same thing happens, let's say, with the dancer's or performer's art), the failure or success has to be immediate. So, I was deeply stirred on the night of the premiere; the emotion I felt, naturally, had nothing to do with the fact that I had already seen the film in a group of four or five persons. I think the circumstance of a hall filled with people in itself creates a special atmosphere. You must have noticed it (I've noticed it very often) . . . There's a book—*La Psychologie des Foules*,[7] I think it's called—about the psychology of crowds, in which it is stated that when people join in a group they react in a more exaggerated way; this is something you must have noticed very often. For instance, if someone tells a joke in a small group, people laugh, but they don't laugh in the same way that five hundred or a thousand people laugh when they hear a joke in a play or a movie. That is, there's a tendency to greater exaggeration, a tendency for everything to happen in a more emphatic manner. And it's strange, the fact that people let themselves go more when they're in a group. On the other hand, a solitary reader, a solitary spectator, seems to have less of a reaction or to react more modestly than when with other people.

F.S. Yes, but the reaction of crowds of people is generally wrong.[8]

J.L.B. Oh, yes. Possibly, the solitary reading of a work is best for its true evaluation. But at any rate, it's a different kind of evaluation.

F.S. You must feel very comfortable working with Bioy Casares, don't you?

J.L.B. Yes. I feel so comfortable that I forget I'm working with Bioy Casares; the one who is really working is that third man whom at times we've called Bustos Domecq and other times Suárez Lynch.[9] And the same thing has happened to me when we three—Muchnik, Bioy, and I—have worked on the development of this film, and now on the other film entitled *Los otros* (The Others) that we're preparing. That is, we forget we're three people and we think with complete freedom. No one feels even slightly put out if a suggestion of his is rejected; no one accepts, either out of courtesy or resignation, what the others say. No, it's as if we three were one single person, a single person working with complete freedom, who has no reason to feel slighted if the others disapprove of an idea of his and who doesn't pat himself on the back if he gets a good idea. I think that if this submersion of the individual personality doesn't occur, collaboration is impossible. That's why collaboration is difficult except, of course, in the case of works of a different nature; two people can work together on a historical or psychological study, perhaps, but I don't think two people, without having submerged their personalities, are able to collaborate in the execution of art.

F.S. Bioy Casares is some fifteen years your junior. I suppose he must have learned a great deal from you.

J.L.B. And I from him!

F.S. That's what I was going to ask you.

J.L.B. It's reciprocal. I think this idea that the teacher is *always* the one who is older is totally false. I don't mean to say the opposite is always the case either. But I know (and for many years I've had my professorship at the University, at the Argentine Association for English Culture, and at the Colegio Libre de Estudios Superiores), I know I've learned a great deal from those who were learning from me; that is, it's a process of collaboration.

F.S. I understand you consider Bioy Casares to be one of the most important writers of the twentieth century.

J.L.B. That's right. I believe a novel like *El sueño de los héroes* (The Dream of Heroes) is a novel that should be translated into many languages. It's truly an extraordinary novel. At first, it appears to be a novel of manners. It's about a group of idlers from the Saavedra area. There's a character who's a sort of teacher to them, a kind of political boss or, maybe, a kind of old murderer, or all of the above. As the characters speak they make errors that might be, that tend to be, that *are* comical. It all seems to be written in the style of a realistic and satirical documentary. But then, as the novel progresses, the reader feels that something else is happening. At last, in the final chapters, the novel works itself up—so to speak—into a nightmare and ends in tragedy. All this has been gradual; you can't tell when this change occurs. On the contrary, very close to the tragic ending there's an episode that's almost comical in nature. All this is handled very skillfully. There's a certain slow pace provided for by the author. I think it's one of Bioy's great books, and I think it's more complex than *La invención de Morel* (The Invention of Morel), for which I had the honor of writing the prologue when it was published.

F.S. Aside from Bioy Casares, what other contemporary Argentinean writer do you think is important?

J.L.B. There is a name, or several names, that seem unavoidable. Manuel Peyrou, especially the short stories contained in *La noche repetida* (The Repeated Night). Manuel Mujica Láinez too . . . And I'm sure there are so many others . . . But these are the first that come to mind. And of course, there are those writers I persist in considering contemporary despite their physical death: Leopoldo Lugones, Ezequiel Martínez Estrada, Paul Groussac . . . But I suppose people think of them as belonging to literary history, that is, as part of a bygone age. And then there's a poet whom it would seem absurd to name [because of his obvious importance]: Enrique Banchs. It's an extraordinary case. Enrique Banchs is somehow the foremost Argentinean poet because of one book—*La urna* (The Urn)—published in 1911. It's a timeless book because it would be just as admirable if it had been published a hundred years before or if it were published a hundred years later. A book that can only be defined by its perfection; I can't find any other possible definition.

F.S. Did you like the fantastic tales of Julio Cortázar?

J.L.B. Yes, I liked them. And there was a little episode . . . Have I told you about it yet?

F.S. No.

J.L.B. I ran across Cortázar in Paris, in Néstor Ibarra's house. He said to me: "Do you recall what happened to us that afternoon on the North Diagonal [i. e. Roque Sáenz Peña Avenue]?" "No," I said. Then he told me: "I brought you a manuscript. You told me to come back after a week and you would tell me what you thought of the manuscript." At that time I was the editor-in-chief of a review, *Los Anales de Buenos Aires*[10] (a now undeservedly forgotten magazine), that belonged to Mrs. Sara de Ortiz Basualdo, and he brought me a short story, "Casa tomada."[11] He came back a week later. He asked me for my opinion and I told him: "Rather than give you my opinion, I'm going to say two things to you: one, the story is at the printer's and we'll have the proofs within a few days; and the other, we've already assigned my sister Norah to do the illustrations." But on that occasion in Paris, Cortázar said: "What

I also wanted to remind you of is that it was the first text I had published in my own country when I was an unknown." And I was very proud of having been the first to publish a text of Julio Cortázar's. Later we saw each other at UNESCO, where he works, a couple of times. He's married—or rather was married—to the sister[12] of a dear friend of mine, Francisco Luis Bernárdez (another poet I should have mentioned, whom I didn't mention because my memory often fails me. There are many writers I admire . . .). Well, as I was saying, I think we saw each other two or three times in our lives, and since that time, he's been in Paris; I've been in Buenos Aires. I believe we profess rather different political views. But I think, when you come right down to it, opinions are the most superficial things about anyone. And besides, I like Cortázar's fantastic tales. I like them better than his novels. I think he has devoted himself too much to mere literary experimentation in his novels, the kind of experimentation I won't say was invented by William Faulkner, but which was abused by him, and which you find in Virginia Woolf too: inversion of the chronological order in the narrative—which for me is the natural order —and of playing free and loose with the order in which the action takes place as he tells his story. But here it seems to me (no doubt this has been said too) that this is what happens deliberately in all detective stories. Because a detective story actually begins with the last chapter, and the entire book has been written for the purpose of getting to the last chapter; this agrees with Poe's aesthetics (and he invented the detective genre), Poe, who said a short story ought to be written for the last line. That is, of course, a way to turn out admirable stories but at the same time, it's a kind of trap in the long run. I think it's possible to write short stories which aren't written for the last line. In any event, I don't know whether anyone had attempted that type of story before Poe, or perhaps before Hawthorne, but I believe stories can be written which are continuously pleasing, continuously exciting, and which don't lead us to that last line out of mere astonishment or mere bafflement.

F.S. What do you think of this current—or maybe not so current now—boom in Argentinean literature; is there something "fabricated" about it?

J.L.B. It's possible that the fact that literature has been commercialized now in a way it never was before has had an influence. That is, the fact that people now talk about "bestsellers," that fashion has an influence (something that didn't use to happen). I remember that when I began to write, we never thought about the success or failure of a book. What's called "success" now didn't exist at that time. And what's called "failure" was taken for granted. One wrote for oneself and, maybe, as Stevenson used to say, for a small group of friends. On the other hand, one now thinks of sales. I know there are writers who publicly announce they've had their fifth, sixth, or seventh edition released and that they've earned such and such an amount of money. All that would have appeared totally ridiculous when I was a young man; it would have appeared incredible. People would have thought that a writer who talks about what he earns on his books is implying: "I know what I write is bad but I do it for financial reasons or because I have to support my family." So I view that attitude almost as a form of modesty. Or of plain foolishness.

F.S. Coming back to an earlier subject, I suppose the list of contemporary Argentinean writers you consider to be of value is in no way an exhaustive roll call. Am I right?

J.L.B. No, no, of course not! My conscience is bothering me at this very moment. Because there's a name—especially if we're talking about poets—that should have been one of the first. I'm referring to the name of the great poet from the Province of Entre Ríos: Carlos Mastronardi. Mastronardi is one of the first writers I met when I returned from Europe in 1921 after a long absence. We became good friends. He told me later that at first he had sought my friendship because he knew that another poet from Entre Ríos, Evaristo Carriego, had been a close friend of the family. So, what he was looking for in me at first was a sort of reflection of Carriego, since I had met Carriego when I was a child, since we had shared the same part of town (the outer fringes of the Palermo district, that Palermo of whose toughs and tenements he sang in *La canción del barrio* [Neighborhood Song] and in "El alma del suburbio" [Soul of the Outer Fringe]). But later we discovered other subjects we had in common. We became close friends and we fell into the curious vice of exploring the city of Buenos Aires. So I remember many evenings and just as many early mornings back then with Carlos Mastronardi, deflowering every nook and cranny of Palermo, the Saavedra flats, the Chacarita district, Alsina Bridge, the long, peaceful streets of Barracas, while continually discussing problems of aesthetics (poetry was a passion with us). Fortunately, we didn't always completely agree. We were able to argue, in a friendly manner always, of course. I've given two courses in American universities. One of them, eight years ago when I went to Texas with my mother. At the University of Texas, in Austin, I gave a course on Argentinean poetry and a seminar on the manifold works of Leopoldo Lugones. And two years ago I went to Cambridge (Massachusetts) where I gave a course on Argentinean poetry and a seminar on Lugones at Harvard University too. Once the course was over, the students had to hand in papers; one girl gave an admirable paper on Mastronardi's admirable, "Luz de provincia." I know many stanzas by heart and many of my students learned them too. I know that through my efforts, boys and girls from Texas and New England now have verses of Carlos Mastronardi running through their minds, verses of "Luz de provincia" and of that poem which unforgettably begins:

> The tall, sorrowful woman
> came out of the south and was dead.
> Fatigue was faithful to her voice . . .[13]

I have a peculiar kind of friendship with Mastronardi, because it's a friendship that is able to dispense with frequent contact. We live near one another (he lives at the Hotel Astoria on the Avenida de Mayo). We can go for months on end, many months, without seeing each other (although nowadays we see each other at the Argentine Academy of Letters). But that doesn't mean our friendship has diminished in the slightest. Not long ago I had the pleasure of proposing Carlos Mastronardi's membership in the Argentine Academy of Letters; he was elected unanimously (we also elected Conrado Nalé Roxlo, a friend of Mastronardi's, on that occasion). I think Mastronardi's case is unusual in the history of literature because even though he's published several volumes (for example, *Conocimiento de la noche* [Acquaintance With the Night]—the title of which brings to mind a poem he didn't know: "Acquainted With the Night," by Frost), even though he's published several volumes—and recently, an admirable book of memoirs entitled *Memorias de un provinciano* (Memoirs of a Provincial), he is still a sort of *homo unius libri* (one-book man); he is still the author of that poem dedicated to Entre Ríos Province, to the nostalgia for Entre Ríos. And I'd say that one of the reasons for Mastronardi's living in Buenos Aires as a recluse and a night owl is that in Buenos Aires he can better feel the nostalgia for his beloved Entre Ríos. And in some way Entre Ríos is mine too, since my father was born in Paraná or, as they used to say in those days, in *el* Paraná (there was also an era in which they used to say *el* Entre Ríos, *el* Azul, and *el* Rosario; I believe those definite articles have now fallen into disuse). I feel a great affection for Mastronardi, a great admiration for his poetry, and I should have mentioned his name in the first place. It's just that after you're past seventy, your memory tends to fade away; that's why my mention of him is a little late.

    F.S. Were you and Martínez Estrada friends?

    J.L.B. It was hard to maintain a friendship with Martínez Estrada. Because he was a person who somehow had given himself over to misfortune, and not only to misfortune but to mistrust. I think Martínez Estrada was a great poet. For example, that poem entitled "Walt Whitman," the one that says:

> If you are in the banner of stars and stripes
> or in the plowshare that virilely turns over the earth,
> or in the milestone that stands watching, like a reproach,
> or in the nuptial colloquy that enlivens the dawn,
> or in the ship's crew arming itself for mutiny,
> or in the herd of buffalo crossing the night . . .[14]

is one of the great poems of the Spanish language. I've dealt with Martínez Estrada quite a bit, especially when he lived in Lomas or in Témperley (I don't remember exactly) and I lived in Adrogué. I used to visit him and chat with him. But later, I began to discover—and the same thing happened to Pedro Henríquez Ureña—that a friendship with Martínez Estrada was difficult because he somehow tended to twist what you had said, to see evil intentions in innocent remarks, and sometimes even in remarks that were nothing but praise. For instance, I published, along with Silvina Ocampo and Adolfo Bioy Casares, an anthology of Argentine lyrical poetry,[15] and in the prologue I said—and not everyone agreed with me—that I believed Ezequiel Martínez Estrada was, at that moment in our literary history, our foremost poet.[16] Later, I noticed he was quite aloof with me. I asked mutual friends about the reason for that obvious aloofness and they told me he felt I had offended him. And he was offended because he had misinterpreted that remark. He said: "I produced a considerable body of literature in prose, and now Borges calls me the 'foremost Argentinean poet'." But he was overlooking the fact—and of course, was purposely overlooking it (because he was a very intelligent man, one of the most intelligent men I've ever known)— that the *Antología* was a *lyrical* anthology. So that there was no mention of any writer's prose. It happened that out of forty or fifty poets, I was merely saying that I felt one of them to be the foremost. And that, nevertheless, was taken by him as an indirect, vicious, and highly labyrinthine way of negating his prose work. You can imagine how hard it is to maintain a friendship with people who take everything in that way. And this isn't the only example I could give you. And then, of course, conversation with him was difficult because you had to be on your toes; you had to try not to make any remark that might lend itself to being twisted like that.

F.S. You had to mind your P's and Q's with him.

J.L.B. Yes, but I believe that even so, Martínez Estrada was such an intelligent man that he managed to turn every bit of praise into an ironic remark or a veiled attack. And he succeeded in doing just that, in any event. I think that led him to a certain solitude in the end. Henríquez Ureña told me the same thing; he told me he had found it necessary to give up his friendship with Martínez Estrada because everything he said was taken the wrong way. I think Martínez Estrada somehow enjoyed torturing himself.

F.S. Now that you mention Henríquez Ureña, were you friendly with him and with Amado Alonso?

J.L.B. Yes, of course. I greatly admire both of them but I've really been closer to Pedro Henríquez Ureña[17] than to Amado Alonso. That doesn't mean I think more highly of one than the other; it simply means that circumstances brought me closer to Pedro Henríquez Ureña than to Amado Alonso. Henríquez Ureña was not a happy man, because he always lived as somewhat of an outsider, an exile. I suspect that in Spain people didn't let him forget that, after all, he was a mere Dominican. Something similar happened to Alfonso Reyes. They didn't let him forget he was a Mexican; they somehow viewed him as an intruder. I know that people here in Argentina weren't sufficiently generous with Pedro Henríquez Ureña. For instance, to limit myself to something that's not important in itself, Pedro Henríquez Ureña was never a full professor of a subject he knew thoroughly: Spanish literature. He was always an adjunct or associate professor. And the full professor—whose name I don't wish to remember[18]—was an Argentinean who also thought of Henríquez Ureña as a mere Dominican.[19]

F.S. Around what date was that?

J.L.B. When you talk to me about dates it's as if you were talking to me about something . . .

F.S. It must have been, I think, around '45, because I think Amado Alonso and others left the country one or two years later.

J.L.B. Well, they *had* to leave the country because the dictatorship dissolved everything they had accomplished. But Henríquez Ureña didn't; Henríquez Ureña died first, of a heart attack, while catching his train at the Constitución Station to get to La Plata to teach his classes.[20] He died suddenly. And it's curious: the last time I saw Henríquez Ureña (it must have happened a week or ten days before he died), we spoke of that admirable poem, that admirable "Epístola moral" which is attributed to an anonymous poet of Seville (I think his name was discovered later; it's something like Fernández de Andrada, but I'm not sure). There's a part of it that reads:

Oh Death! Come silently,
as is your wont to come on the arrow . . .[21]

And I told Henríquez Ureña that the arrow metaphor had to originate with some [ancient] Latin poet. Henríquez Ureña answered that it seemed very probable to him and that he was going to look into the matter. Of course in that era, in the seventeenth century, no one spoke of plagiarism; on the contrary, it was quite honorable to bring an image or a line of poetry from one language to another. That is, it was honorable to demonstrate that the vernacular tongues were as good as the classical languages which everyone knew and admired. The fact is that a week or ten days after that conversation with Pedro

Henríquez Ureña—I think it was on the corner of Azcuénaga and Santa Fe, more or less at two o'clock in the morning, death came to him in that manner; it came to him *silently*, as is its wont to come on the arrow. And even up to this very moment, I haven't been able to ascertain the origin of those verses and I don't know whether Henríquez Ureña ever discovered it before death took him by surprise that way. He was a man of extraordinary intelligence and extraordinary courtesy. On this last point, his timidity might have had an influence.

F.S. I believe he was one of the first to read Ernesto Sábato's manuscripts.

J.L.B. Of course, because Sábato possibly was a disciple of Henríquez Ureña, since Sábato studied in La Plata. Still, I don't remember having spoken of Sábato with Henríquez Ureña. Pedro Henríquez Ureña and I used to speak very often about the Modernist Movement, which seemed very important to the two of us (and still does to me). His brother Max wrote that *Breve historia del modernismo* (Brief History of Modernism),[22] an admirable book, it seems to me, in which emphasis is placed on the fact that the Movement came out of America and later reached Spain; a curious situation when you consider that the Movement took its inspiration from Hugo, from the Symbolists, from Edgar Allan Poe . . . Nevertheless, that Movement came out of America, crossed the Atlantic, and reached Spain afterward. We used to talk about that and all kinds of literary subjects, American poetry too, about his personal recollections of New York, where he lived for a long time and with which I wasn't familiar at that time, and about the arts in general.

F.S. What did you do on October 17, 1945?[23]

J.L.B. The truth is I don't remember. The truth is that I thought, and I still think, it was a kind of farce; I don't think anything *really* happened. Because if the Dictator had been kidnapped and had been rescued by a mob—as the story went later, it's very strange—given the vengeful nature of the man [Perón]—that the matter was never investigated. I think it was carried out a bit scenographically and that, naturally, no one believed in it. That is, it's something that is more real now than at the very moment it took place.

F.S. What did the Perón years represent for you?

J.L.B. The truth is that I tried to think as little as possible about politics. Still, in the same way a person with a toothache thinks about that toothache from the very minute he wakes up, or a man whose woman has left him thinks about that woman as soon as he passes from sleep to waking, that's the way I used to think every morning: "That man, whose name I don't wish to remember, is in the Presidential Mansion." And I would feel sad, and somehow I also felt remorse because I'd think that not doing anything or doing very little . . . What could I do? Mention him in the lectures I gave, always with ridicule (I couldn't do anything else; I didn't feel capable of doing anything else). All that saddened me. On the other hand, I felt the fact that my mother, my sister, one of my nephews, and many of my friends were in prison during that time was sad, but honorable too.

F.S. That didn't happen to you?

J.L.B. No, they merely assigned a detective to me, and I ended up being his friend. He would patiently wait for me every morning when I left my house on Maipú Street. At first, I had a good time leading him on long, purposeless walks through Buenos Aires. Finally, I realized it was a silly game. I spoke to him; the fellow told me he was really an Anti-Peronist but was doing his job. Then we came to a sort of tacit agreement. I said to him: "Look, the truth is I'm not involved in any conspiracy and I give you my word not to do anything that could compromise you, so if you like, we can dispense with this system unless you should happen to wish to talk to me." And he said: "Well, let's see each other, not every day, but every other day and let's talk about all kinds of things, including politics, since we both think pretty much the same way." I don't remember what that man's name was.

F.S. How did you react to the Revolution of '55?[24]

J.L.B. I was misinformed that night. I thought [Admiral Isaac F.] Rojas was going to bombard the city that night. We had been advised to evacuate the area that was going to be bombarded. That afternoon I had received a book on Icelandic literature. I thought: "This house may be destroyed but I'm going to save this book." The truth is I could have saved three or four books, but I thought that if it was a symbolic act, it would have to be *one* book. The idea that it was a book of whose value I was ignorant and not a cherished old book struck me funny. Then I went with my mother to my sister's place. We weren't very far away since my sister lived on Juncal Street, a block from the five corners. Then I went out for a walk (I didn't know what had happened; I was thinking that the bombardment was being delayed) and suddenly found myself in front of the house of a dear friend of mine: the writer, Susana Bombal. I went upstairs. I noticed something strange in the maid's face. Susana arrived at that moment, embraced me, told me something that now would sound theatrical but which wasn't at the time, because the theatrical is fitting in emotional situations. She said something like: "My noble friend!" She asked me if I had eaten breakfast. The truth is that I hadn't, but I lied; I told her I had eaten. And then I began to understand what had happened; the Revolution had been successful and I hadn't known it. Then I immediately telephoned home. I also called the home of Adela and Mariana Grondona (they had already heard the news). Next I remember a confused, happy morning, a rainy morning. I remember having walked along Santa Fe Street, having run into Ortiz Basualdo's daughter—the daughter of that very same lady who published the *Anales de Buenos Aires,* in which I published that first text of Cortázar's—and, after we had lost each other in the crowd, I found her on Libertad Street and suddenly it turned out that we had come back to Santa Fe Street, that I had already lost my voice from shouting "long live our homeland!" so many times (I think no one shouted a single "down with" that day). In addition, I was soaked to the skin because it was raining buckets and I hadn't realized it, I was so carried away with patriotic enthusiasm. And I recall that other morning that brought so many of us together in the Plaza de Mayo. I remember I was with Cecilia Ingenieros, José Ingenieros' daughter, and came upon my mother and sister there, and they better than I had known prison under the Dictatorship. I remember that joy, that impersonal joy. I recall that no one thought of his or her own fate at that moment; each one thought: "our homeland has been saved." And now that new dawn has been somewhat obscured . . .[25] we can say it, can't we? But I believe that in the end we won't be unworthy of it.

F.S. How would you reconcile the idea of democracy and free elections with the fact that Peronism usually wins out at the polls?

J.L.B. That would be an argument against democracy and free elections. I suspect that the form of government is very unimportant, that what's important is the country. Let's suppose there were a republic in England or that there were a monarchy in Switzerland; I don't know whether things would change much. Possibly they wouldn't change at all. Because the people would still be the same. So I don't think a particular form of government is any kind of panacea. Maybe we place too much emphasis on the form of government; maybe the individuals are what's important.

F.S. I'm going to bother you with a dilemma which you'll probably find atrocious. Supposing you had to choose between a Peronist government and a Communist government, which of the two would you pick?

J.L.B. It's not a dilemma because they both would be the same thing. Besides, the Peronists are used by the Communists. So I don't see any difference between them. Except that perhaps . . . Yes, of course. Actually I think there is a difference and it's this: I can imagine myself a Communist—although, of course, I'm not a Communist and I despise Communism, but I cannot imagine myself a Peronist. A Peronist is a person who pretends to be a Peronist but who doesn't really care about it at all, who does it for his own personal ends. It's possible for a Communist government to be a sincere government. On the other hand, a Peronist government would be a government of scoundrels. I believe there would be that in favor of Communism. There are people who sincerely believe in Communism. I—at least under the Dictatorship—didn't know anyone with the nerve to say "I'm a Peronist," because such a person would have realized he was making a fool of himself. Instead he would say: "Peronism is convenient for me because I derive such-and-such advantages from it." That's why a poster there was at Corrientes and Pasteur struck me funny. It said more or less: "Doctor So-and-So, a disinterested Peronist, holds forth on the divorce regulations at his classical law office at such-and-such a number, Corrientes Avenue." And there was this photograph of him in his office, with his books and his inkstand. It's comical; there's an obvious contradiction between "Peronist" and "disinterested." And then there's that expression "holds forth," that sounds like something out of Bustos Domecq. Ha, ha, ha! The poster was pasted to the wall and I was sorry I couldn't tear it down to keep it as a kind of document, you know?

F.S. How do you think anyone takes it into his head to become a dictator?

J.L.B. It really seems a childish idea, don't you think? I believe the idea of giving orders and being obeyed is more to be associated with a child's mind than with that of a man. I don't think dictators generally are very intelligent people. Fanaticism can lead to it too. Take Cromwell's case, for example: I think he was a Puritan; he was a Calvinist and believed he had every right. But in the case of other more recent dictators, I don't think they've been motivated by fanaticism. I think they were impelled by histrionic zeal, by the desire for applause, for being obeyed, and perhaps by the mere childish craving for publicity, which is a craving I don't understand.

F.S. What differences do you see between Rosas and Perón?

J.L.B. I think they're probably very much alike. And I can talk with some impartiality on this because I'm a relative of Rosas. I think Rosas must have represented in his time a calamity equal to that of Perón.[26] Of course, Rosas had to be more cruel than Perón because he had to deal with people who were tougher than our modern Argentineans. But I think Perón, who didn't hesitate to use the electrified cattle prod, wouldn't have hesitated to use the snag-toothed knives of the nineteenth-century death squads either. It's just that Rosas happened to live in a more savage era, and that obliged him to be more cruel, and therefore more spectacular too, than Perón. Since even now we think of Perón's era as a sad epoch and we think of Rosas' era as a sad, but also picturesque era. It's true the country was picturesque then and isn't any more. It's a colorless country nowadays, more than anything else, but back then it wasn't. Outside of a few cities like Buenos Aires, Córdoba, Rosario, Montevideo (there's no reason not to include it too), it was a country that was just what Sarmiento said it was. He said: "The Argentine Republic and the Republic of Uruguay are one cattle ranch."[27] And whatever was not a ranch was Indian Country.

F.S. What is your opinion of the work being carried out by those who are revising our history in order to rehabilitate Rosas' image?

J.L.B. A cousin of mine married Ernesto Palacio who was, along with Irazusta, one of the initiators of Revisionism. Of course, he admired Mussolini. He admired Fascism and wanted to find a sort of vernacular Mussolini here; that turned out to be Rosas. He asked me to join the Juan Manuel de Rosas Institute. I told him that in spite of certain distant family connections I have with Rosas,[28] I thought he was an abominable person. Besides, my entire family is Unitarian . . .[29] Besides, there's Sarmiento to think about . . . And finally, I told him I didn't understand why they were putting themselves to so much trouble to come to a predetermined conclusion. If one revises something, I think he should revise it honestly. One shouldn't say: "I'm going to revise such-and-such facts to arrive at such-and-such a conclusion." And I told him that if they had decided the Unitarians were a lie, they had no reason to investigate anything because they already knew they were going to arrive at the conclusion that Rosas was a patriot, that Rosas was a great man, that Rosas wasn't the coward we used to think he was, etc., etc. . . . But it wasn't necessary to investigate anything if they already knew the conclusion beforehand. It's very odd for one to go to so much trouble to go down that route when one already knows what the goal is. Why not come directly to the conclusion without feeling any need to back it up with argumentation?

F.S. Do you think it paradoxical that the same people that produced a Schopenhauer also produced Hitler?

J.L.B. The German people certainly is, along with the English people, one of the most curious peoples on Earth. For example, it produced Schopenhauer, as you said; it produced German music. And at the same time, it is easily led by a man like Hitler. Wells believed humanity would be able to save itself through education. This idea could be parodied with a couple of lines of Eliot. They went something like this:

Where is the wisdom we have lost in knowledge?
Where is the knowledge we have lost in information?[30]

Of course, I don't see any way to acquire wisdom other than by means of knowledge and even information. Still, if there ever has been a country in which there was information and in which there was knowledge, that country is Germany. And yet that country allowed itself to be deceived by the really puerile arguments of Hitler. The truth is that I can't discover any reason for that contradiction. Yet that contradiction exists. What you also find in the Germans—and what you certainly do not find in Schopenhauer—is respect for authority, a sort of Chinese respect for hierarchies, the attachment of great importance to people's titles. I think we are much more skeptical than the Germans in that sense; we understand that hierarchies are the result of circumstances and that circumstances are the result of chance. On the other hand, the Germans, who have produced skeptical philosophers, do not as a rule produce skeptics. The Germans accept authority. And an opinion like Schiller's, "Die Weltgeschichte ist das Weltgericht," which is to say, "the history of the universe is the Final Judgement,"[31] seems to correspond to an admiration of success which I think is typically German. This would be the opposite of that statement by an English thinker who said: "Nothing fails so much as success."[32] On the other hand, you see that the Germans are admirable soldiers so long as they believe in the possibility of victory, but apparently are incapable of fighting for a lost cause. The Spanish Fleet, after the Cuban débacle, sailed out for the specific purpose of having itself sunk. On the other hand, you probably recall that the German Fleet surrendered to the English Navy in 1918 when it realized it would be useless to fight.

fourth
conversation

Dostoyevsky and Chesterton — Censuring Calderón — Poe's
Image — South American Destiny — The Kafka Translation —
The Spanish People — Borges' Languages — Dante Alighieri —
Advantages of Poor Memory — John Kennedy — Verne, Wells,
and the Astronauts — Horacio Quiroga's Faults — Written Humor,
H. Bustos Domecq, and Carlos Argentino Daneri — Carlos de la
Púa's Dictionary

F.S. It's easy to find opinions on many English, German,
French, or Spanish writers in your essays. On the other hand,
it's very difficult to encounter any opinion on Dostoyevsky or
Tolstoy. Consequently, I'd like you to explain, for this book of
ours, how you view those two writers.

J.L.B. When I was nineteen years old, I thought Dostoyevsky was perhaps the greatest novelist in the world, and it
annoyed me when other writers were discussed and considered
on a level with him. Later, the same thing would happen to me
with the Tolstoy of *War and Peace*. But it didn't take long for me
to realize that this admiration of mine didn't entail the desire
to read any works of theirs other than the ones I had already
read. For example, I've read and re-read *Crime and Punishment* and *The Possessed*. Then I had to give up on *The Brothers
Karamazov*, a family which never managed to hold my interest,
and I finally realized I had no desire to read any other books by
Dostoyevsky.[1] On the other hand, I saw that what I really felt
like reading were authors I thought of as inferior at that time.
For instance, I tried to read every line written by Chesterton,
and yet I would have been indignant—at that time—at anyone's comparing Chesterton with Dostoyevsky. Maybe what

happened to me with Dostoyevsky is that I was slowly beginning to realize that his characters were all very much alike and there was something unpleasant in that continual idea of guilt, and that I didn't find in him what I really like most in literature: the epic.

F.S. Once, in an informal conversation, you gave me an opinion on Calderón de la Barca that doesn't coincide with the one usually seen in books on the history of literature. I'd be most grateful to you if you'd repeat it.

J.L.B. I believe I said that Calderón de la Barca was something the Germans invented. I believe I said the title of the work *La vida es sueño* (Life Is a Dream) was responsible for his being considered a metaphysical poet. One finds this in Schopenhauer's *The World as Will and Idea*, and Schopenhauer speaks of the oneiric essence of life (I think it's something like "das traumhafte Wesen des Lebens," but I won't answer for the accuracy of my quotation). Now then, I think that phrase can be interpreted in two different ways. For example, when Shakespeare compares life to a dream, what he insists on is the unreality of life, the fact that it's hard to draw a line between what we dream and what we live. On the other hand, I think that in Calderón's case the phrase has a theological sense: "life is a dream," in the sense that our lives, our waking days, don't correspond to *the* reality, but only to a small part of reality, the sense that what is real is Heaven and Hell.

F.S. That's pretty much Manrique's idea, I believe.

J.L.B. I think so too. I think Calderón's idea is a religious one, or rather, a Christian one. I think Calderón was stressing the fleeting quality of life, comparing it with the fleeting quality of a dream. As for Calderón's versification, I find it excessively poor; this must be, perhaps, because I haven't read him well, but the fact is I can't tell one character from the other, and I think the theatrical mechanism is too obvious in his works. The same can be said for the entire classical Spanish theater. I know I'm speaking heresy, but as I'm going to be seventy-two years old, I think I can afford to be a little heretical, don't you?

F.S. While we're on the subject of theater, what do you think of Lope de Vega?

J.L.B. I see Lope de Vega as an admirable poet. With reference to his theater, one has to accept so many conventions. And the plots—those games of confusion—I find them so uninteresting . . .

F.S. Among your favorite authors (Wells, De Quincey, Chesterton) are some whom the critics generally don't consider to be major figures. Conversely, you negate Calderón, for example, who is generally admired by everyone. What explanation would you give for this fact?

J.L.B. I attribute this predilection of mine to the fact that I judge literature in a hedonistic manner. That is, I judge literature according to the pleasure or emotion it inspires in me. I've been a professor of literature for many years and I'm not unaware that the pleasure caused by literature is one thing and the historical study of that literature is another. Take Edgar Allan Poe's case, for example. I believe Poe, as a poet, is mediocre, a sort of miniature Tennyson. As for Poe's short stories, each one of them judged separately, except perhaps *The Narrative of Arthur Gordon Pym*, suffers, I think from truculence, from bombast . . . Nevertheless, Poe's importance is considerable if we judge it historically. We could say that what today is called *science-fiction* originated with Poe. It's evident that Poe is the inventor of the detective genre and that there are stories of his—"The Purloined Letter," for example—that perhaps haven't been surpassed. It's evident that Baudelaire was inspired by Poe, that the Symbolist Movement was inspired by Baudelaire, and that Paul Valéry was inspired by Symbolism. That is, you can't deny the historical importance of Poe, but that doesn't mean that each one of his stories, poems, or essays is especially admirable. One might oppose what I've just said with the fact that the image left by an author is more important than each page he's written, and no doubt, that image of misfortune, of arrogance, of a brilliant imagination that Poe has left is also one of his works. Furthermore, literary historians often seem to me to be individuals enamored with mere information, to come back to a subject we dealt with some days ago. And as for literary movements, I think they're mere conveniences for the historians and, in the best of cases, are stimuli for the author to produce his work.

F.S. If you had been born on August 24, 1899, not in Buenos Aires but, shall we say, in London, or Paris, or Berlin, what kind of writing career would you have had?

J.L.B. It's obvious that the circumstances would have been different. Had I been born in a country with a rich and ancient culture, my work would possibly have passed unnoticed. On the other hand, I've been lucky enough—literarily lucky, so to speak—to be a South American, and that has resulted in an exaggeration of the merits of my writing. And now that I say that, it brings to mind an analogous case; I'm thinking of Groussac. Had Groussac remained in France, he possibly would have been a good French writer, a good French historian, but he wouldn't have been outstanding. On the other hand, it was his fate to be an exile, to write in a language he didn't like, to have to renovate the style of that language, to live in a still pretty primitive Argentina. And all that permitted him to be, I don't know whether it would be correct to say "greater," but certainly more beneficial for his contemporaries and the surroundings fate had allotted him.

F.S. One morning, on our way downstairs, you mentioned to me that the Argentinean writer usually is superior to his work, the reverse of what occurs in the case of the European writer. You told me you had met Camus.

J.L.B. Yes, and that he hadn't impressed me one little bit. On the other hand, it seems that it's his work which has impressed . . . Now, I believe that possibly, this is a lazy country, this is a fundamentally skeptical country. That is, a country that doesn't demand much of anyone, and that produces a tendency for us to write inferior material. Because we know that success is—especially now—a mechanism to be manipulated. On the other hand, in other countries each writer finds himself compelled to give his all.

F.S. Aside from Spanish and English, which were your mother tongues, what other languages are you able to read?

J.L.B. When I had my sight, I was able to read German and could enjoy German literature.[2] A few days ago we spoke of Germany; I would venture to say Germany has produced, among so many other things, something I think is superior to everything else it has given us, even thinking of some admirable poets, even thinking of Heine, or of Angelus Silesius, or maybe Hölderlin, and that something is the German language, which I think is extraordinarily beautiful, which I think is made for poetry.

F.S. I seemed to notice in your translation of Kafka's *The Metamorphosis*, that you differ from your usual style . . .[3]

J.L.B. Well, that's due to the fact that I'm not the author of the translation of that text. A proof of this—in addition to my word—is that I know something about German; I know the work is entitled *Die Verwandlung* and not *Die Metamorphose*, and I know it should have been translated as *The Transformation*. But, since the French translator preferred—perhaps as a salute from afar to Ovid—*La Métamorphose*, we subserviently did the same thing here. That translation has to be—I have that impression because of a few turns of phrase—the work of some Spaniard. What I did translate were the other stories by Kafka which are in the same volume published by Editorial Losada.[4] But, to simplify matters—maybe for merely typographical reasons, they preferred to attribute the translation of the entire volume to me, and used a perhaps anonymous translation floating around out there.

F.S. It's often said that you find Spaniards tedious and that you find Spain and its literature tedious. Do you concur with that statement?

J.L.B. No, I don't concur with that statement. I think Spain is an admirable country; or rather, a collection of admirable countries, especially when I think of Galicia, when I think of Castile—here my enthusiasm is somewhat dampened—when I think of Andalusia. I believe the average Spaniard—what they call "the man in the street" in English—is one of the finest men in the world, especially from the ethical point of view. I have never known a cowardly Spaniard; I could almost say I've never known a dishonest Spaniard. On the other hand, Spanish literary figures—with certain exceptions—do not elicit any admiration on my part. For instance, if I had to compare the Spanish with other ethnic groups, I would say that Spaniards are, in general, ethically superior to the others. For example, I've never met a stupid Italian, I've never met a stupid Jew. On the other hand, I've met very few Spaniards whose intelligence has especially impressed me. That is, I would speak of an *ethical* superiority of the Spanish.

F.S. Coming back to the subject of languages, from which we've strayed, what memories do you have of your experiences as a Latinist?

J.L.B. Memories that are clearer than my memory of the language itself, of Latin. It saddens me to think I devoted six or seven years to the study of Latin, that I came to enjoy Virgil's poetry and the prose of Tacitus and Seneca, and that now all I have left of all that Latin are a few Latin phrases. But—I don't know if I've already mentioned this—I think having forgotten Latin is in itself a kind of possession since Latin teaches us a kind of economy, a kind of strictness, a love for the sententious. And I believe this is beneficial in the handling of other languages. And at this point I recall a line of Robert Browning. It goes:

Latin, the language of marble.[5]

I think this refers not only to the fact that Latin inscriptions are common, but to the fact that the Latin language seems made to be carved in marble. It's as if there were a natural affinity between those two entities, between Latin and marble.

F.S. And it never occurred to you to study Greek?

J.L.B. No. For one thing, there's a reason I usually give when I'm asked why I don't know Greek; it's that there are so many people who already know it for me. But I don't know if that's the real reason. The truth is that I've felt attracted—just a moment ago I spoke of my admiration for German, and everyone knows how much I admire English—I've felt attracted instead to the Germanic languages. At present, after nine years of having devoted myself to Old English, I'm studying Old Icelandic, a language related to Anglo-Saxon. Besides, I'm about to become seventy-two years old and am not able to undertake the study of languages whose roots are different from those of the languages I already know. For example, I would have liked to know Hebrew, but I know it's beyond my present capabilities. When I was a young man, I would have been able to do it. I know that essentially the same thing is happening to me with Old English and with Old Icelandic. I know I won't ever possess them, but I also know that this sort of slow voyage toward the impossible somehow is a pleasure. And I think I said all this in one of the poems of my book, *Elogio de la sombra* (In Praise of Darkness).[6]

F.S. Haven't you ever felt a kind of remorse when reading the Greek classics in translation?

J.L.B. No. I used to think about this the same way I thought about Arabic. Not knowing Greek and Arabic allowed me to read, so to speak, the *Odyssey* and *The Thousand and One Nights* in many different versions, so that this poverty also brought me a kind of richness.

F.S. What kind of impression did your first reading of *The Divine Comedy* make on you?

J.L.B. I undertook that first reading in rather anomalous circumstances. I was employed in an unassuming little library in Almagro Sur. I was living in the Recoleta district. In order to get to work, I had to take two long streetcar trips—I believe it was car line 76,[7] I'm not sure—and I came upon an edition of *The Divine Comedy* in Italian and English, done by Carlyle[8]—not by the famous Thomas Carlyle, but by a brother of his. It was a bilingual edition. I would read it on the streetcar: first, a page in English; I'd try more or less to retain it, and then I'd read the corresponding page in Italian. Besides, I've found that if someone knows Spanish, he possesses Portuguese to some extent and, although to a lesser degree, Italian. Well now, when I came to the Island of Purgatory, at the South Pole (in the second volume), I realized I could now do without the English version and that I could continue to read in Italian. Later, I was so dazzled by this book that I felt all the rest of literature to be haphazard; I felt it was the product of chance compared to *The Divine Comedy*, in which everything appears—and doubtless is—premeditated by the author. Later, I acquired Italian editions of the *Comedy*. I remember Scartazzini's edition; I remember—I read this one later—the edition by the Jewish-Italian scholar, Momigliano; I remember Grabher's edition; I remember Torraca's; I remember Steiner's . . . And I discovered that *The Divine Comedy* has been so admirably annotated, line by line, that one can read it almost without knowing any Italian. Dante, in a letter to Can Grande della Scala, said his *Divine Comedy* could be read in four different ways. This reminds me of what Scotus Erigena said; he said the Holy Scriptures were "like the feathers on a peacock's tail, made up of an infinite number of colors." Later, I found that in the opinion of certain Jewish theologians, the Holy Scriptures have been written for each and every one of their readers; the Book has been foreseen by God, and the reader has been foreseen by God. This would also give us an infinite number of possible readings. On the other hand, I think the Spanish translations of *The Divine Comedy* essentially are involved in an error: the error of having us believe that Italian differs greatly from Spanish. I believe that any Argentinean, any Colombian, any Spaniard, should undertake reading *The Divine Comedy* in the original. It's true he'll have to put up with some inconveniences at first; it's also true that he'll find it infinitely rewarding. I know there are people who instinctively put off reading *The Divine Comedy* because they feel there's something essentially false in the work. A great French poet, Paul Claudel, said that the scenes awaiting us on the other side of death will probably have no relation to the Purgatory and Paradise dreamed up by Dante. Instead, he imagines a Hell that's a kind of—so to speak—vertiginous Luna Park [a huge Buenos Aires sports arena like Madison Square Garden]. Now then, I think this objection is completely devoid of merit. I don't think Dante believed that Hell corresponded to his nine circles, Purgatory to that sort of artificial mountain composed of terraces, and Heaven to some vague but radiant place in which one converses with the saints. No. Dante himself, in the course of the *Comedy* says no one can anticipate God's decisions; no one can say now that "A" will be damned and that "B" will be saved. And yet, throughout *The Divine Comedy* we see reprobates and penitents and the blessed whose exact names are given. How can this be explained? I think Dante invented that structure, that topography—or rather, geography—of the three kingdoms for literary purposes. One tiny fact would be enough to justify this thesis of mine: as one reads *The Divine Comedy*, one would say the other world is populated exclusively with biblical characters, by characters from the Classics and, above all, by Italians. This anomaly must have been sensed by Dante. What happened is that Dante selected for each of the sins, of the degrees of penance, or of the virtues, a typical character, and that character had to be one already known to the readers, a character the readers' imaginations would easily accept. And one of Dante's commentators—I think it was his own son[9]—said that what Dante had intended was to represent the condition of the just through the metaphor of Heaven, the condition of those who repent through the metaphor of Purgatory, and the condition of the sinners through the metaphor of Hell. That is, the very vividness, the very incomparable vividness of *The Divine Comedy* has resulted in our reading it as if it were a book of imaginary geography. And this fact, which at first was in its favor, now militates against it. But I believe it suffices to realize this simple fact—the fact that when Dante died, he didn't expect to find himself in any of the three regions dreamed up by his imagination. This simple fact suffices to allow us to enjoy *The Divine Comedy*, and I can tell you *The Divine Comedy* constitutes for me one of the most vivid literary experiences I have had in the course of a lifetime devoted to literature.

F.S. Did the religious value of *The Divine Comedy* come through to you, or did you simply give your attention to its literary value?

J.L.B. What has least interested me in *The Divine Comedy* is its religious value. That is, I'm interested in the characters, I'm interested in what happens to them, but the whole religious concept, the idea of rewards and punishments, is an idea I've never understood. The idea that our personal conduct could be of interest to the Divinity, and the idea that my personal life— I've already said this at some time or other—could deserve eternal punishment or eternal reward seems absurd to me. The ethical part of *The Divine Comedy* is precisely the part in which I've never been interested.

F.S. I would imagine that you, whose work is so filled with memorable verses, must know by heart many lines of poetry written by others.

J.L.B. Yes, but they'd be a very different kind of poetry. They'd be, most likely, the verses of minor poets. Besides, I've noticed that lately my memory is failing me, and I can see this in my study of Icelandic. I recall that when I began to study Old English, I was able to remember long passages, that is, passages of fifteen, twenty, or thirty lines, and that now, with Icelandic, I can't do that any more. And yet, if we're talking about my memory, I remember what I've read better than what I've lived. Or, to be more accurate, of everything I've lived through, what I've read is sharper and more real for me. On the other hand, if I think about my own life, I tend to forget. Especially in everything relating to chronology. I don't know now how long ago I was in Israel for the first time, for example. I wouldn't be able to state the exact date of my stay in Texas or in New England. I don't know exactly what year I was in Scotland and in Denmark and, nevertheless, those countries left a deep impression on me. And if I had to write my autobiography, that autobiography would be filled with circumstantial errors. I was preparing a revision of my first book, *Fervor de Buenos Aires* (A Passion for Buenos Aires), and I added one or two explanatory notes. And a friend of mine, Norman Thomas di Giovanni, discovered that the data I had provided were false. For example, I said that such-and-such a passage is to be found in such-and-such a book published on such-and-such a date; and it turned out the passage belonged to a different book published on an entirely different date. But forgetting particulars doesn't bother me since, after all, life supplies us with an excess of particulars. And I sensed that some time ago in a poem entitled "La noche que en el Sur lo velaron" (Night Death Watch on the Southside), in which I say, with some perhaps excusable exaggeration, that the night frees us from one of the greatest sources of anguish: the tediousness of reality. That is, by day we make our way through a city composed of details, and at night, in the middle of the night, especially toward the outlying districts, we make our way through a simplified city, a city with the simplicity of a chart or of a dream.

F.S. How did you receive the news of John Kennedy's assassination?

J.L.B. I received that piece of news with an emotion I wouldn't know how to analyze. I remember I was walking through this neighborhood, the one in which the National Library is; I heard someone say: "Kennedy's dead." I assumed this

"Kennedy" was some Irishman in the neighborhood, and later, as I was entering the Library, someone said to me: "He's been killed . . . !" And then I understood, from the tone in which he said it, whom he was talking about. And I recall, during that same day, having stopped in the street with people I didn't know and who didn't know me, and our having embraced each other as a way of expressing what we were feeling.[10] That day there was a sort of communion among men, as there was also that Sunday on which the first men landed on the moon. That is, there was the emotion over what had occurred, and there was also the emotion of knowing that thousands of people, millions of people, maybe all the people in the world, were feeling great emotion over what was occurring. With the difference that in Kennedy's case we felt that something tragic had happened and, on the other hand, in the case of men landing on the moon, I think we all felt it as a personal joy. I would go even further; I would say I felt a kind of personal pride, as if I had somehow been one of the creators of that prodigious feat, since we've all looked at the moon, since we've all thought about the moon.

F.S. Now that you've just mentioned the voyage to the moon, do you think that voyage is responsible for cheapening the value of Jules Verne's imagination, or that of Herbert George Wells, for example?

J.L.B. No. I think people understand that they had imagined certain things and had to situate them somewhere, and they situated them on the moon. On the other hand, nowadays they would have chosen a different place. As for Verne, it's strange that his name is always associated with these things, since Verne was a very peculiar man. Because he indubitably had imagination; at the same time, that imagination doubtless was more timid—shall we say—than that of Wells. You must remember that in the two volumes[11] of Verne's voyage to the moon, he's opposed or unwilling to have his explorers reach the moon. The projectile in which they live falls into the Pacific Ocean, unlike Wells' sphere which reaches the moon. I think by the third chapter of Wells' *First Men in the Moon*, which corresponds to 1901, the two friends—one of whom turns out to be a traitor—have already set foot on the moon. On the other hand, Verne refused to go that far. And I recall having read an anecdote—I don't know if it's true—in which Jules Verne was outraged by Wells' inventions. And he said: "Il ment!" ("He's lying," he said, with French logic). I also remember that Wells used to boast that everything imagined by Verne would or could come true, and that, on the other hand, what he himself had dreamed up wouldn't ever come true. Still, I'm sure Wells would have been glad to have been proven wrong, and that he would have been as excited as we were to see there actually were "first men in the moon."

F.S. What merit do you attach to the short stories of Horacio Quiroga?

J.L.B. I don't know if you know that my family is of Uruguayan background. My grandfather Borges was born in Montevideo, before the Great War. And I'm related to families like the Haedos, the Melián Lafinurs,[12] and others. Now then, after having made this statement, I'm going to make bold to declare that the merits of Horacio Quiroga's short stories seem to me—I won't say *absolutely*, because that adverb shouldn't be used—but seems to me almost nil. I think Horacio Quiroga is a sort of Uruguayan superstition. I think Quiroga's style is deplorable; I think his imagination is impoverished, and furthermore, when I read Quiroga's stories, what happens is that I can't believe in them, and I think this is very serious. I think that while we're reading a story we must believe in it. And besides, here I must bring to mind an observation made by Novalis. Novalis said there are many passages in books which are appropriate to the reader and not to the author. On the other hand, Horacio Quiroga appears not to have sensed that difference. Horacio Quiroga marvels at what he is recounting. Horacio Quiroga uses words such as *atrocious, terrifying*, maybe *stupendous*, which are appropriate to the reader, not the author.

That is, Horacio Quiroga is a reader who admires his own work too much.

F.S. Nevertheless, you once told me you thought Lugones' fantastic tales in *Las fuerzas extrañas* (Strange Forces) were good; these are stories in which it's hard to believe too.

J.L.B. Yes . . . But how can we compare one writer with another? Lugones—if we accept his baroque style—was a great writer. Quiroga, a very mediocre writer; a writer capable of unbelievable clumsiness. For example, it must be some four years ago that I read a story by Quiroga, "A la deriva" (With the Current), in which there's a man who, I believe, is paddling up-river and is bitten by a snake. Well then, in that story you can't tell what pertains specifically to the account and what pertains to the man's customary activity. That is, that tale is filled with unnecessary ambiguities which derive from the literary clumsiness of the author. As for Quiroga's poetry, it appears to be a sort of parody—an involuntary parody—of the poetry of Herrera y Reissig, which itself seems to be a parody.[13] For example, a while ago you asked me if I remembered any poetry. Well then, I remember some of Horacio Quiroga's verses. I remember these lines:

. . . of the green Japanist vases . . .

This isn't something I've made up. And then, a poem about a naval battle, "Combate naval," in which they talk of:

the navy vanguard of cadets.[14]

That was something he published in *Los arrecifes de coral* (The Coral Reefs), and he allowed it to be reprinted afterward. It's possible I've written poetry which is no less ridiculous, but then I've been wise enough to be ashamed of it and to erase it. And now that I've mentioned Herrera y Reissig, I don't know what kind of bad luck pursued him, because all he had to do was to mention a ruby for the reader immediately to think of a piece of glass, or to mention gold for one to think of just any kind of metal at all. However, I think there was a certain passion in him, that Herrera y Reissig was a passionate person, even if it was the passion of literary madness, don't you think?

F.S. Would the style of Roberto Arlt be similar to that slightly careless style of Quiroga's?

J.L.B. Yes, except that behind Roberto Arlt's carelessness I feel a sort of strength. A disagreeable strength, of course, but strength nevertheless. I think Roberto Arlt's *El juguete rabioso* (Mad Toy) is superior not only to everything else Arlt has written,[15] but to everything written by Quiroga.

F.S. In the same way, I suppose you must have found Manuel Gálvez' novels tiresome.

J.L.B. Yes, but it was a different kind of tiresomeness. It's rather the tiresomeness of the dull, of the mediocre, a more peaceful tiresomeness and, therefore, one that's more bearable. Then too, it's true I never got very far in reading him.

F.S. Now, I'd like you to give me your opinion of Arturo Cancela's humorous stories.

J.L.B. There's a story by Arturo Cancela I like very much; it's called "El destino es chambón" (Fate is a Bungler).[16] But, in general, I think humor in writing is a mistake. Of course, this means negating a good part of Mark Twain's work. I believe humor is something that arises out of conversation, and that it's excusable and even agreeable in conversation. And this brings Macedonio Fernández to mind. Macedonio Fernández' jokes were admirable at the moment in which they were told because they arose out of the conversation. But then he made the mistake of writing them down, of interweaving them, and he reached a sort of almost unreadable baroque style.[17] I believe that in time written humor will disappear and humor will remain only as an embellishment born of conversation. But all this doubtless is heterodox . . . What I like best in humor is absurdity, above all, logical absurdity. For example, there's a joke—I don't know whether we've taped it yet—that was made up by a cousin of mine, Guillermo Juan Borges: "There were so few people at the concert that if one more person were missing, there wouldn't be any room for him." But he came up with that because he was in Macedonio's sphere of influence. Macedonio was such an intelligent man that he obliged everyone who spoke with him to be intelligent. No one could be a fool while speaking with Macedonio Fernández . . . This, of course, is related to the idea of mental telepathy. I believe mental telepathy is not an unusual phenomenon, but something that occurs continually. For instance, on what are love and friendship based? They're not based on what a person says because we all say more or less the same thing. They're based on the fact that we feel an affinity behind the words the other fellow utters. It has happened many times in my life that I'll attend a gathering and meet—let's say—two people. One of them makes some intelligent and keen observations. The other one limits himself to a smile and silence, or simply to silence. Nevertheless, as I leave the house I think: "'A' is an imbecile; 'B' is an intelligent man." 'A' had said some intelligent things; 'B' hadn't said anything. And later I discover I hadn't been wrong, that there's a form of communication which goes beyond words. And this indubitably occurs with a literary work too. There are authors who, line for line, page for page and, perhaps, book for book, are not especially admirable. Yet one ends by admiring them because all that leaves us with a total image that we find pleasing.

F.S. However, despite your just having negated the value of written humor, you yourself have been guilty of indulging in it through Carlos Argentino Daneri and through Bustos Domecq.

J.L.B. Yes, but my having committed something doesn't make it any less blameworthy.

F.S. But why, then, despite your being conscious of its being blameworthy, did you do it?

J.L.B. I believe that whenever one does wrong, he knows he's doing wrong. Still, he does it. I believe that no one thinks his own behavior is exemplary. And this holds true in literary matters as well. In the case of Bustos Domecq,[18] Bioy Casares and I felt we shouldn't allow ourselves to be led by him. Nevertheless, we did allow ourselves to be led by him. In the case of Carlos Argentino Daneri[19]—and here I'm the one who needs defending—I think the joke is excusable because it's included in a context[20] which is tragic, perhaps, and certainly fantastic. Which is to say, Carlos Argentino Daneri is a comical character but is, after all, part of a text that is not comical, or at any rate, that doesn't aspire to be comical, but which aspires to be a fantasy. And it's quite possible that it's my only piece of humorous aggression, so I don't feel too much remorse over it.

F.S. Could Carlos Argentino Daneri, perchance, be the archetype of the mediocre Argentinean writer?

J.L.B. No. He's a friend of mine—whose name I don't wish to recall[21]—who read the story, who didn't recognize himself in it, and who liked it and congratulated me. When I outlined that character, I knew I was not committing an act of treachery; I knew I could do it with complete impunity since possibly no one would note the resemblance, not even the model himself.

F.S. I think I recognize, in Dr. Mario Bonfanti, the character in *Seis problemas para don Isidro Parodi* (Six Problems for Mr. Isidro Parodi), Arturo Capdevila or Enrique Larreta. Am I right?

J.L.B. No. I admire Capdevila, and as for Larreta, maybe he's reflected in another character in the book, in Gervasio Montenegro. And there's a remark once made by Larreta on some page of *Seis problemas para don Isidro Parodi*, except that it's used jocularly there while Larreta wrote it in a totally serious vein. But the truth is I've read Larreta very little, I've never been greatly interested in his work, and I'd rather not speak about it at all than speak ill of it.

F.S. Are you satisfied with the tangos and milongas you composed with Piazzolla[22] and the milonga you composed with José Basso?[23]

J.L.B. I'm pretty much satisfied with the lyrics. And I'm more satisfied with Basso's music than with Piazzolla's. But the fact is that I have no musical propensity at all and my judgment is of no importance.

F.S. Is there, on that record in which you've had a hand, *Catorce con el tango*, any tango by another of the writers who took part which you particularly like?

(Without saying a word at this point, Borges indicates, by means of gesture, infinite doubt.)

F.S. The one by Petit de Murat, perhaps?[24]

J.L.B. The one by Petit de Murat . . . refers, I believe, to Güiraldes and a newspaperman who had acquired a dictionary of underworld slang and whose name was Carlos Muñoz, alias *Carlos de la Púa*. I think there's a line that's repeated several times: "Dance a tango, Ricardo!" And I think it's a curious slip. People generally say "grab yourself a tango," don't they?[25] But in general, we writers make mistakes when we try to write in underworld slang.

fifth
conversation

The Brave Tango and the Sentimental Tango — Truco — The
Brothels of Maldonado Creek — A Gaucho-Style Poem by Arturo
Jauretche — Radicals and Conservatives — Hipólito Yrigoyen —
Francisco López Merino's Farewell — Vicente Fidel López and
Bartolomé Mitre — Director of the National Library — The Druids
and the Druzes — Eduardo Mallea — Editions of *Martín Fierro*

F.S. We know you'd prefer the tango not to have lyrics . . .

J.L.B. I don't like the tango as a song. It's true the first tangos had lyrics, but in general, they were obscene lyrics, lyrics
made simply for mnemonic ends to help remember the music.
Besides, the tango's having lyrics has led to the dramatics in it,
which is precisely what displeases me. Because I prefer, shall
we say, the tradition of the gaucho troubadours, that is, a way of
singing with a certain indolence, with a certain indifference, of
sometimes relating bloody events innocently, as if they didn't
realize what they're relating. And I believe that makes them
more effective, too. On the other hand, especially with Gardel
and after Gardel, there's a tendency for each tango to be a little dramatic and sentimental episode which customarily con-
cludes with a sob . . . And, personally, I find that distasteful;
possibly it's just an old-line Argentinean's prejudice.

F.S. And in the specific case of Homero Manzi, do you like
his tangos? For instance, the tango "Sur"?

J.L.B. The tango "Sur," yes. It has a good opening line:

Sur, paredón y después . . .
(Southside, a wall and then . . .)

At the same time, there are some phrases that obviously don't ring true, that betray, I won't say the man of letters, but certainly the pseudo man of letters. For example, in a tango I believe is his there's mention of "the wind of the outer limits." This is a phrase that no neighborhood tough would have used. In the first place, because the idea of the "wind of the outer limits" is a phony idea, and in the second place, because the slum dweller doesn't boast of living in the outer limits; he says "I'm from the Retiro District" or "I'm from the Montserrat district," or from wherever he may be. But the term "outer limits" is an entirely sophisticated one that no neighborhood tough would ever have used:

> Me la nombran las estrellas
> y el viento del arrabal
> (The stars and the wind
> of the outskirts [of the City]
> whisper her name to me)

One can plainly see it was written by someone from the affluent downtown area, who has sentimental ideas concerning the *compadres* and is totally unfamiliar with the songs of the people, which never would have contained such lyrics. Now, Homero Manzi (I've met him; his name used to be Manzione) possibly knew absolutely nothing about that ambience or, and this is more likely, didn't care about verisimilitude.[1]

F.S. You mention Juan Muraña in more than one poem;[2] did you ever meet him?

J.L.B. No, I never met him. But I've met people who knew him. For instance, I've met Marcelo del Mazo and don Nicolás Paredes. Muraña was a well-known person in the Palermo district; I believe he was Paredes' bodyguard. He was a teamster and, so I've heard, he finally began to drink heavily and one night fell from the front seat of a cart and broke his skull on the cobblestones of Las Heras Street. And he was the most famous knife fighter. He and Suárez the Chilean. This is so much the case that almost all the anecdotes about hoodlums which are told or—rather—which *were* told in that district, are assumed to be about him. But we must remember the French phrase "on ne prête qu'aux riches" (one lends only to the rich). So that any act of bravery was felt to be "right" for Muraña, who was famous for his bravery and for his skill with the knife. The only skill he had, because I don't think he was an intelligent man; naturally, there's no reason for him to have been.

F.S. On a previous occasion you spoke nostalgically about the café La Paloma, where they used to play *truco*. In addition, you've written a poem concerning *truco*.[3] It would seem to indicate that this card game represents something very gratifying in your life.

J.L.B. Yes. It represents some very pleasant hours. Above all because I think *truco* is superior to other games. Of course, not to chess or to bridge, but certainly to poker. And the fact is that even if you play for money (which is quite frequent), the money you win isn't important. A proof of this is in the fact that no one says "I won so many pesos at *truco*" but rather "I beat So-and-So." That is, there's a disinterested rivalry in *truco*. Furthermore, *truco* seems to be made for killing time more than anything else; that's why it's a very slow game, which poker is not. And that's only natural because poker—I think—was invented by adventurers in the American West, people looking for gold who wanted to get rich quickly. On the other hand, *truco* is a game for people who have very little or nothing to do; it's a game of the pampas, of the hill country, of the ranches. I would compare it with drinking *mate*,[4] in the sense that it's more a pastime than anything else.

F.S. Is *truco* of Argentinean, Uruguayan, or Spanish origin?

J.L.B. That presents some difficulty. There's a Spanish card game called *truquiflor*. Now, in Spain I've spoken with people who knew that game and, according to what they told me, it doesn't resemble ours. There are two varieties of *truco*: the one we play in the Republic of Argentina and the one played in Uruguay, which is called *truco-up-to-two*, and which is played with a "show card." That is, once the cards are dealt, you take out a card and that card's suit is the "show." If you have (for example, let's say the "show" is in diamonds), if you have a four of diamonds, you can beat the ace of spades with it. There's a curious fact, and it's that in that long and, in general, langorous poem written by Ascasubi, *Santos Vega o Los mellizos de "La Flor,"* a game of *truco* is described, one that supposedly was played before the May Revolution. And that game of *truco* corresponds exactly to *truco-up-to-two*.[5] There can be two explanations for that: we can think that Ascasubi, who spent so much time in the Republic of Uruguay and who was there during the Great War, during the siege of Montevideo by Oribe's Whites, learned that brand of *truco*; we can also suppose that this form of *truco* is the older form of the game, and that the game we play (which in the Republic of Uruguay is called *blind truco* or *Buenos Aires truco* and is the one learned by young boys before learning the other one) is a simplification of the other one. Now, I never learned to play *truco-up-to-two*, which is the one played in Uruguay and which is more complicated, because that matter of the show card comes up throughout the game, so that, for example, there can be *flowers* of a higher number than . . . I believe the highest *flower* is 47, I'm not sure. Well, whatever.

F.S. At this point in time, when the old City is disappearing before our eyes, I'd like you to pinpoint the spots in which were located those brothels you mentioned on a different occasion. The ones that were around Maldonado Creek: on which streets in the Palermo district?

J.L.B. Those brothels were off Maldonado Creek. Naturally, I was a child and I couldn't have had any direct experience in this. But I've spoken with a great many neighborhood people, among them for example, Alfredo Palacios, who used to live just around the corner. So that they were on the Creek, that is, what now is Juan B. Justo Street, where the Creek is piped up. And I think—because I've spoken with people from the Villa Crespo district and the Flores section too—that Maldonado Creek had a tendency—I don't know why or, precisely, because it was a pretty unpleasant drainage ditch—it had a tendency to produce a pretty unpleasant type of population, of humanity. Or in any case, there were certain people who sought out that obviously poor district. And in regard to the street names, those brothels had to be very close to the streets I think are still called Humboldt or Darwin, those streets with the names of naturalists; or, on this side of Pacífico, on Godoy Cruz Street. More or less around there. And I believe that kind of house of ill repute and those underworld types of the native as well as Calabrian brand, were found all along Maldonado Creek. Of course, it's quite a long creek, quite a long ditch; because I've seen Maldonado Creek in the Villa Luro district, where there are those streets with names of poets, those streets called Virgil, for example, or Homer . . .

F.S. The other day, while leafing through some old books, I came across one from 1934, Arturo Jauretche's *El Paso de los Libres*, which had . . .

J.L.B. A prologue of mine.[6] Yes, but why did you think it strange? I think there are some very nice lines of poetry in that book. And I think the fact that we're now on opposite sides of the political fence[7] doesn't mean I'm now going to judge the poetry he wrote at that time to be bad. That is to say, we don't see each other at present (I wouldn't say I'm avoiding him, because my eyes are so bad that I couldn't avoid anyone), but, in short, we're quite far apart; he became a Peronist, etc. . . . But there are some good lines of poetry in that book. I met him through Enrique Amorim, because after the Uriburu revolution[8] he emigrated to Uruguay. Enrique Amorim is married to a cousin of mine, Ester Haedo, and I met him there. He asked me to write a prologue for the book and, as it had some really nice poetry in it, there were lines which at times brought to mind Hilario Ascasubi's tone—one of the gaucho-style poets I most admire—I wrote that prologue and I'm not ashamed of having written it.

F.S. No. The thing is, in the first place I wasn't aware that Jauretche had written poetry. I knew him instead as a politician . . .

J.L.B. Well, and I didn't know he was now a politician either. I haven't had any news of him for quite some time . . .

F.S. You didn't know he was a candidate for the Senate some ten years ago?

J.L.B. Jauretche . . . ??? Well, I don't know. I haven't seen him for I don't know how many years. I haven't had any news of him. And I'm not even acquainted with anyone who knows him either. Occasionally his name comes up in a vague kind of way . . . But, anyway, I have no reason to be ashamed of having written the prologue for a book of verses which I considered to be good and which perhaps, if I were to re-read it, would still seem good to me.

F.S. In *La fundación mítica de Buenos Aires* (The Mythical Founding of Buenos Aires)[9] you have a line that says: "The stable boys were sure in their opinion: YRIGOYEN." That line, does it have a pejorative connotation or one of solidarity with respect to what the stable boys' opinion was?

J.L.B. I'm glad you asked me that. I was a Radical[10] [Unión Cívica Radical: a populist party], I was affiliated with the Radical Party. But I was affiliated with it for totally illogical reasons: simply because my maternal grandfather, Isidoro Acevedo, was a close friend of Alem's. So that I was a Radical [Populist] by tradition. But then, when the Radicals came to power and I realized they were a calamity for the country,[11] I thought it was absurd for me to continue being a Radical for reasons we might say have to do with piety, with ancestor worship, reasons like these of the Chinese or genealogical type . . . And then, some four or five days before the elections, I went to see Hardoy and told him I wanted to join the party he was running.

This has its own prehistory too. Once, I was engaged in conversation with a writer and she suddenly said to me: "You, as a Conservative, say this." And I told her: "No, I'm not a Conservative: I'm a Radical." And she said: "No, no. You are essentially a Conservative." And I realized she was right. This was one of the reasons that led me to join the Conservative Party. Besides, I realized that whenever I spoke with Conservative friends of mine, I agreed with them on everything. So I joined the Conservative Party a few days before the elections. Hardoy tried to advise me against it; he told me it was absurd, they didn't have the slightest chance of winning, and I made this remark. I told him: "A gentleman is interested in lost causes only."[12] And he said to me: "Oh, well! In that case I won't say another word."

F.S. But this wasn't at the time you wrote the prologue for Jauretche . . . It must be about ten years ago. Isn't that right?

J.L.B. No, it must be even less, I suppose . . .

F.S. It must have been in '63, around the election won by Illia.

J.L.B. Yes, exactly. And afterward I realized I had done well to join the Conservative Party. But I've never taken an active part in politics, not even when I was a Radical. Naturally, when I joined the Conservative Party, it was announced and I probably made some kind of speech. Or rather, not a speech; I must have spoken at some committee meeting saying that the eras of greatest honor, of greatest prosperity, of greatest dignity in this country were under Conservative governments. But my political activism has been limited to that. The truth is I don't have any calling for politics.

F.S. How did you view the mysterious figure of Hipólito Yrigoyen?

J.L.B. I never met him. My family, yes; they were friends of his. I didn't ever meet him, and the curious thing is that Yrigoyen cultivated that air of mystery. It was even said that he continued to conspire during his presidency as he had done all his life. And, contrary to another ruler whose name I don't wish to remember [Perón], I think he was not a very intelligent man but still a man of great integrity. For example, he kept living modestly in a walk-up apartment in a house on Brasil Street. He wasn't a snob as other dictators were, the ones who would frequent the Colón Theater and who were fond of luxury. On the contrary; belonging to a good family, he was never interested in attending high-society gatherings; his daughter wasn't interested in buying her clothing in Paris; he didn't like to see his picture everywhere. In other words, he continued to be a modest and obscure Argentinean gentleman while at the same time being the President of the Republic as well. And now that we're speaking of Yrigoyen . . . —I don't know whether we've already recorded a remark of his . . . It seems a group of people went to see him after the election that made him president— unfortunately for him—for the second time. Then he answered them with a remark that turned out to be prophetic: "I'm going to say to you, as the old-time Balvanera denizens used to say (Balvanera—The Eleventh [of September]—was his district and that's where Alem was political boss): 'Things have always gone so badly for me that when they go well it scares me.'" And he was right as rain. Because if Yrigoyen had lost that election, we would remember him or he would have left us the memory of a good president or, in any case, of an honorable man (well . . . , he still is an honorable man), but, in short, it would have been better for him not to have been elected for a second term. Besides, he accepted Uriburu's revolution. That is, when he became aware that the country didn't want him to be president, he didn't press the matter.

F.S. What memories do you have of Francisco López Merino, to whom you dedicated a poem?[13]

J.L.B. I have very precise memories of López Merino. We were close friends. I know he committed suicide because he had discovered—by means of an X-ray he had to take to a doctor (he opened the envelope on the way from La Plata to Buenos Aires)—that he had tuberculosis. And tuberculosis—

I believe this happened in 1928—was at that time an incurable disease. So he made his decision: suicide. I saw him for the last time at home. We were living on Quintana Avenue[14] between Montevideo and Rodríguez Peña. Panchito López Merino— that's what we affectionately used to call him—would come to our house more or less once a week or once every couple of weeks. Then he would have to travel that long route from the Recoleta district to Constitución Station in order to catch the train which would take him to La Plata. He had eaten with us. My father had retired early and López Merino said: "I want to say goodbye to Dr. Borges." My father had already gone to bed, and I knew my father was the kind of man who fell asleep as soon as his head touched the pillow (once he told me that he always would think about an imaginary country before going to sleep—he didn't want to give any details about that country—and that he would then begin to dream of that country and would fall fast asleep). So I knew my father was already asleep. Mother told Panchito that Father was asleep and that she would tell him the next day that López Merino had said goodbye to him. López Merino, who was a very courteous person, nevertheless said, with a certain obstinacy which did not exclude courtesy: "I *want* to say goodbye to Dr. Borges" (that's what he used to call my father). So I went upstairs to my father's room, awakened him and told him López Merino wanted to say goodbye to him. My father was a bit surprised. López Merino came in and said to him: "I want to say goodbye to you, Dr. Borges." He clasped his hand and left. And then, some ten days later he committed suicide. Then we understood why he had wanted to say goodbye. He wanted to say goodbye because that goodbye was not a mere ceremony or a frivolous ritual; he was really *saying goodbye*. That is, he knew he was going to kill himself; if not, there's no way to explain his obstinacy. I remember he committed suicide on Mother's birthday, May 22.[15] There was a little group of friends at our home, we were drinking champagne, it was raining buckets, and in the midst of all that they said something to me about the newspaper *El Mundo*. They gave me the news, they asked me to tell some anecdote about him, and then the thing that always happens when people mention your friends happened: you have a very precise mental image of him but it's hard to transmit that image or to compress it into an anecdote.

F.S. Is there a particular newspaper you especially enjoy reading?

J.L.B. No. Anyway, I never read the newspaper.

F.S. Not even before [your blindness]?

J.L.B. I've never read newspapers. And I've never read them because through some perversity of mine I'm more interested in what occurred a long time ago than in current events. I remember I was in Geneva when the First World War broke out, and I was studying ancient history at that time. And I thought, with complete innocence—it's true I must have been fourteen or fifteen years old—I thought, "How strange it is that suddenly everyone is now interested in history; how strange that no one's interested in the Punic Wars or the wars between the Persians and the Greeks, and that now everyone is so interested in contemporary history." In addition, it occurred to me that possibly it's not so easy to know what's going on right now. And now a remark of Macedonio Fernández' comes to mind—I'm always coming back to Macedonio Fernández— "Historians, they're as knowledgeable about the past as we are ignorant about the present." This is so much the case that when men landed on the moon I didn't know it was going to have an emotional effect on me. I thought it was an event that had to take place sooner or later, given the aims of science. And yet, I already began to be anxious a week before it happened; I already began to fear it would fail. And then, when men actually stood on the moon, I felt an emotion we might call intimate, personal. And at the same time, I was cheered by the idea that probably every person in the world was feeling the same thing, that we all felt personally happy and proud of the fact that it had taken place, that somehow we all were participating in that accomplishment, that it wasn't simply those who had planned it and those who were executing it. All men have looked at the moon, have desired such an event, and must have felt satisfied about it. And then I thought—I might possibly have been mistaken—that the fact that three men reached the moon is something that is able to unite all men. Because it's the kind of feat that belongs to all mankind, going beyond the fact that they may be Americans or Hungarians or Chinese or what have you . . .

F.S. I once read in *La Prensa* that if you had to select three works by Argentinean writers, one of them would be Vicente Fidel López' *Historia*. Why do you like that book so much?

J.L.B. It's very hard to explain a liking for something.

F.S. Then compare him with Mitre.

J.L.B. I feel there's an intimacy in López' tone which is not present in Mitre. And I believe López' work wasn't created as a pedestal on which to place a particular personage. On the other hand, the *Historia de San Martín* or the *Historia de Belgrano* were created a bit as pedestals, as monuments; they were made for the purpose of exalting particular individuals. On the contrary, I think Vicente Fidel López takes in a whole Argentinean tradition and takes in the defects as well.

F.S. How, where, and when did you meet Victoria Ocampo?

J.L.B. I had given a lecture—or rather, I had written it and someone else had read it (I didn't have the courage to speak in public)[16]—on *El idioma de los argentinos* (The Language of the Argentineans). A very exaggerated title, of course; nowadays I would speak rather of an Argentinean *intonation* of Spanish, of an Argentinean *respiration* of Spanish, but not of a different language, and Victoria agreed with that lecture. Then she wrote me a letter and came to our house—it was when we lived on Quintana. And later she was extraordinarily kind to me. When *Sur* magazine was founded, she included me on the editorial board. The first issue of *Sur* carried an engraving done by my sister and an article of mine on the works of Ascasubi, which I felt had been unjustly consigned to oblivion. And from that time on we've been the best of friends and, in addition, I owe to her and to Esther Zemborain de Torres my becoming the director of the National Library. And to Dr. Dell'Oro Maini too; and to Ricardo Sáenz Hayes. Because in 1955, after the Liberating Revolution, when it was necessary to find people who were completely above suspicion of being Peronists, they thought of me. Esther Zemborain did; then she spoke with Victoria Ocampo, who spoke with Dr. Sebastián Soler, and they immediately started a campaign to have me appointed Director of the Library. I learned of this; I spoke with Victoria and told her I'd be biting off more than I could chew with the National Library and that he who grabs too much, holds on to very little—this is not a very original metaphor but, anyway . . . — and that why didn't they try to have me made director of the Library of Lomas de Zamora, for example, which would permit me to live in Lomas—which is a town I like very much. Victoria told me: "Don't be an idiot," and, as a matter of fact, after some time had passed (the Revolution was in September), on October 17 I went with a group of writers to greet General Lonardi. I remember that day. We were in the Plaza de Mayo. Under the watchful eye of the security detail there were timid Peronists on the corners who, from time to time, lifted their eyes to the sky looking for a black airplane,[17] according to what was being said. I thought: "How strange. I'm going to enter the Presidential Mansion. The Dictator isn't in the Mansion, and for the first time in my life I'm going to shake hands with a President of the Republic . . . All this is like a dream." Then the President received us. I was the last one. Each one of us had to tell his name. When I told him mine, General Lonardi said to me: "Director of the National Library, if I'm not mistaken?" And then Mujica Láinez or someone else said: "We are most gratified to hear you speak those words, your Excellency." I was dumbstruck. Later we left. I went home; my mother said: "How did it go for you with the President?" "Fine," I said. Then she said: "They've just spoken to you about the Ministry of Education." "Oh," I said, "you must be talking about what Lonardi said to me." Then I explained to my mother that he had told me I was the Director of the Library. That night, my mother and I went out for a walk. We came here to Mexico Street, and my mother said to me: "Well, now that you're the Director, why don't you go in? Let's take a little look around inside to see how everything is." And, because of some kind of superstitious fear, I said: "No, I'd rather not go in until I'm told it's all right." And, the fact is I didn't go in. On the following morning I was advised by the Ministry of my appointment and that I could take charge of running the Library. And the whole thing was a friendly plot dreamed up by Esther Zemborain de Torres and then organized by Victoria Ocampo and by other friends of mine.

F.S. Weren't you in the habit of coming to the Library before becoming the Director?

J.L.B. I was very timid. I'd come to the National Library often, but actually the only book I would read was the *Encyclopaedia Britannica*. And it was the *Encyclopaedia Britannica* because I knew that this encyclopedia was on the side shelves and I wouldn't have to order it from a librarian. So that it was all so much simpler. I'd take out any volume at all of the *Encyclopaedia* (which was an old edition; which is to say, one of those editions not made for reference but for reading, with long articles; anyway, I didn't care—so to speak—whether the statistics were *à la page* or not; I'm not interested in those things), and I recall a most agreeable evening in which I acquired quite a bit of information on the Druids and on the Druzes, who naturally were neighbors in the pages of the *Encyclopaedia*. So I came to the Library quite often and, of course, I knew that Groussac was the Director. But I never had the courage to approach Groussac because I knew he had an abrasive personality, was an unpleasant person to deal with, and that in short, conversation with him would have been disagreeable. He was a person who lost his temper easily. Besides, Groussac felt like an exile. Groussac thought his true destiny was to be a great French writer and it pained him to have to live here, at the end of the world. He wrote that sentence: "One can be famous in South America and still be unknown" in which his nostalgia for France and a certain bitterness can be noted.

F.S. Eduardo Mallea is on the editorial board of *Sur* too.

J.L.B. Yes. I met Mallea . . . I'll tell you how exactly. One Sunday a group of young writers came to the house. I must have been four or five years older than they, and the difference was rather important in those days. Now it isn't important because things even out with time. Those writers were: Leonidas de Vedia, Carlos Alberto Erro, Saslavsky, Mallea, and someone else. They told me they were going to found a review and asked me for a poem. I felt very proud and, at the same time, somewhat fearful that once the poem was read it would be rejected unanimously. But anyway, I received them, gave them the poem and, some days later, they told me I could correct the proofs, which I thought was a good sign . . . I think the publication was called *Revista de América*,[18] and three or four issues came out. That visit made me feel very proud.

F.S. Do you like Mallea's novels?

J.L.B. Yes, especially a short novel entitled *Chaves*, which I think is the best thing he's written. And then a short story, whose name I don't recall,[19] about a man who is jealous, before the fact, of a stranger, and then more or less provokes his wife's adultery; something like a more complex version of Cervantes' "El curioso impertinente."[20] Now Mallea is, as I am, a timid man, so that we've become friends, although not close friends. That is to say, I think highly of him, I know he thinks highly of me, but we don't see each other very frequently. And it's the same situation with me and Carlos Mastronardi, and this is an even stranger case. Because I would say Carlos Mastronardi is my closest friend, except I don't want to use the word *closest* because it appears to exclude others, and I certainly don't wish to exclude Adolfo Bioy Casares, for example, or Manuel Peyrou. The fact is that I might see Carlos Mastronardi twice a year, and that doesn't dim our friendship in the least.

F.S. Did you know Carlos Alberto Leumann?

J.L.B. Yes, but not very well.

F.S. Have you read any of his works?

J.L.B. I read some novel of his; it didn't interest me. And I read the prologue of an edition of *Martín Fierro*. In that prologue there's an affirmation which I think is untenable. He says he's used, for that edition of *Martín Fierro*, the same procedure used by Lachmann, I believe, for publishing the *Nibelungenlied*, the *Song of the Nibelungs*. Now then, I don't know what the connection is between bringing out a critical edition of a series of medieval manuscripts and the task of republishing a book originally published in Buenos Aires in 1872. Furthermore, I don't think Leumann had any knowledge of the field. And now that we're talking about *Martín Fierro*, I believe there's an edition of *Martín Fierro* with really valuable notes, and which is certainly not the one put out by Tiscornia (since Tiscornia limited himself to a series of imaginary parallels between the Spanish picaresque novel and gaucho-style poetry), but is that of Santiago Lugones—a cousin, I believe, of Leopoldo Lugones—a man who really knew the field and who places *Martín Fierro* in *Martín Fierro*'s own milieu and not in a milieu that might have been that of seventeenth-century picaresque Spain, which has absolutely nothing to do with life in the Province of Buenos Aires in the eighteen seventies, in the era of Indian raids and log forts.[21]

F.S. Some days ago we had spoken about the film *Martín Fierro*. Later there was the premiere of the film version of *Don Segundo Sombra* . . .[22]

J.L.B. I haven't seen it. Now, all the reports I've heard are excellent and at the same time, I think it's very hard to make a film based on a book which is almost a series of sketches of manners. Because, outside of the growing friendship between the old cowpoke and the boy, I don't know what novelistic action it has.

sixth
conversation

The Dictionary of Argentinisms — The First Book — Evaristo
Carriego — Twentieth-Century Spanish Writers — Alfonso Reyes
— The Library and the Poultry Market — Benefits of Peronism —
Discépolo's Fame — Conan Doyle: The Kittens and the Loaves —
The Strawberry Roan — *Facundo* vs. *Martín Fierro* — The Cheshire
Cat — Kafka and Henry James — The Short Story and the Novel

F.S. Why do you dislike poems such as "El general Quiroga
va en coche al muere" (General Quiroga Goes to His Death in
a Carriage)?

J.L.B. The poem—let's use that term—"El general Quiroga
va en coche al muere" now seems to me a kind of decalcomania.
I don't even know how I had the nerve to write a poem on a
subject that had already been definitively treated by Sarmiento,
who invented Facundo Quiroga—more or less.[1] I exaggerated
its gaucho flavor when I wrote it, and had to modify that in later
editions.[2] For example, I had written:

> las ánimas en pena de fletes y cristianos
> (both broncos and baptized like unshriven souls)

Later, as I re-read it, I thought that business of *broncos and bap-
tized* came across like a man of letters attempting to sound like
a gaucho, and so I changed it to "de hombres y de caballos"
(men and horses), which I thought was more natural. In addition, I think that poem has one essential defect: it was written to be picturesque, which is to say it was written from the
outside. On the other hand, I believe there's another poem of
mine—with an analogous theme, a poem on the death of Fran-

cisco Narciso de Laprida, entitled "Poema conjetural" (Conjectural Poem)—in which we have a historical theme minus any overabundance of ponchos, mustangs, and all the other devices of the Buenos Aires writer when he wants to sound like a gaucho, and which is written the other way around; that is, I try to feel what the man felt, might have felt, or must have felt. That poem, like another—which I believe is even worse, if it's possible to imagine anything worse—"La fundación mítica de Buenos Aires" (The Mythical Founding of Buenos Aires), is the exercise in picturesqueness of a fledgling writer, and I've always thought it strange that anyone might take it seriously, except as mere entertainment.

F.S. Then you mean it was difficult for you to come to your present linguistic convictions.

J.L.B. Yes. The truth is that to reach the point of writing in a more or less uncluttered manner, a more or less decorous manner, I've had to reach the age of seventy. Because there was a time when I wanted to write in Old Spanish; later I tried to write in the manner of those seventeenth-century authors who, in turn, were trying to write like Seneca—a Latinized Spanish. And then it occurred to me that it was my duty to be Argentinean. So I acquired a dictionary of Argentinisms and devoted myself to being a professional died-in-the-wool Argentinean to such an extent that my mother told me she didn't understand what I had written because she wasn't familiar with that dictionary and because she spoke like a normal Argentinean. And now I believe I've come to write in a more or less straightforward manner. I remember something George Moore said that impressed me. Wishing to praise someone, he said: "He wrote in an almost anonymous style." And I thought that was the greatest compliment an author could be given: "He wrote in an almost anonymous style."

F.S. Then it's obvious that between the *Historia universal de la infamia* (Universal History of Infamy) and . . .

J.L.B. Well, the *Historia universal de la infamia* is written in a baroque style, but it was done as a kind of joke, you see? A not very amusing joke . . . , but, in short, I couldn't think of anything else to write.

F.S. Of course. Personally, I enjoy reading *El Aleph* but not the *Historia universal de la infamia*.

J.L.B. Oh, yes; of course, there's a major difference. The *Historia universal de la infamia* was written by a beginner and *El Aleph* was written by a man with some literary experience and who was mature enough to stop playing certain games, to stop indulging in certain kinds of mischief or pranks.

F.S. How did you feel when you saw *Fervor de Buenos Aires* (A Passion for Buenos Aires), your first book, on the market?

J.L.B. The expression "on the market" is exaggerated because I didn't stock the bookstores with it; I didn't think anyone could be interested in what I was writing. But I recall that I was very excited when I held a copy in my hands. Why that was so is a mystery to me, because after all, there isn't much difference between a manuscript and a book in print, and even less between a typewritten copy and a book in print—although what I actually handed in was a manuscript. Nevertheless, that difference does exist. Because that was my first book, and things make a deep impression when they occur for the first time. As for prizes, people have been very generous with me; I've won important literary prizes, and none has impressed me as much as that Second Municipal Prize for Literature in Prose I was awarded in 1928,[3] because it was the first prize I ever won.

F.S. Did you ever receive any literary advice, in your youth, that turned out to be especially useful for you?

J.L.B. Yes. My father gave me that advice. He told me to write a lot, to discard a lot, and not to rush into print, so that the first book I had published, *Fervor de Buenos Aires*, was really my third book. My father told me that when I had written a book I judged to be not altogether unworthy of publication, he would pay for the printing of the book, but that it was each man for himself and I shouldn't ask anyone for advice. Besides, I was too timid to show anyone what I was writing, so that when the book appeared, my family and friends read it for the first time. I hadn't shown it to anyone and it wouldn't have occurred to me to ask for a prologue either.

F.S. What was Evaristo Carriego like?

J.L.B. Evaristo Carriego was a fellow who was very sure of his talent—*too* sure of his talent, I think—since I remember that he became indignant once when someone declared that Lugones, Almafuerte, and Banchs formed the "triumvirate" of Argentinean literature. He would have liked to scratch out Lugones and put himself in that place. He used to say that Lugones wasn't a poet. The fact is that Carriego had acquired an overly sentimental concept of poetry and felt this hypersentimentality was absent in Lugones.

F.S. And obviously, Carriego's ambition was excessive.

J.L.B. It was an absurd ambition, of course. Now, I don't think he owed anything to Lugones; it would have been better for him if he had owed something to Lugones. He started out as a disciple of Almafuerte and of Rubén Darío; he was a friend of Almafuerte and used to visit him in La Plata. I had a photograph of Mas y Pi at home; Mas y Pi was a journalist who used to sign his name "+ y Π"[4] and was a contributor to the *Nosotros* review . . . The photograph had been taken in Almafuerte's house, which was then on I don't know what street in Tolosa or in La Plata—somewhere out there, anyway; Tolosa is a suburb of La Plata, you know . . . Carriego was a person who was very much interested in the military and above all in everything having to do with Napoleon. And I recall one time he came to the house. They talked about the battle of Waterloo, and I remember that my father and Carriego explained the battle to us using the wineglasses, the demitasse cups, the bread basket, and all that in such a way that we could follow the battle.

F.S. The essays you published in 1932 in *Discusión* ...
Would you write them all over again with those same concepts?

J.L.B. No. I don't recall what those concepts were, but it
would be very sad if I hadn't progressed at all, wouldn't it?

F.S. Well, to use a concrete example: let's say the article on
Quevedo that appeared in *Otras inquisiciones* (Other Inquisitions) ... Do you feel differently now?

J.L.B. Yes, I believe I overly admired Quevedo. And there
are two men who cured me of that excessive admiration: one
was Adolfo Bioy Casares, and the other was Quevedo himself,
whom I've tried to re-read and who now seems to me a writer
who is overly conscious of what he's doing. Besides, I think
there's something rigid, dogmatic, in Quevedo. At the same
time, there's a fondness for silly puns—he shares that fondness
with Miguel de Unamuno too. At present, my admiration for
Quevedo is very limited ... It's curious: at that time, I thought
Lugones was superior to Darío and that Quevedo was superior
to Góngora. And now, I think Góngora and Darío[5] are much
better than Quevedo and Lugones. I believe there's a certain
innocence in them, a certain spontaneity, that the other two
didn't have; those two took everything too seriously.

F.S. You think there's spontaneity in Góngora?

J.L.B. In some sonnets, yes. Of course, in his later works,[6]
no: in the *Soledades*, in the *Polifemo* (I think these works are
part of—I'd say—almost a sort of literary perversion). But I
think there are sonnets—the sonnet "A Córdoba," for example,
and others—in which there is spontaneity. And that's something you seldom find in Quevedo.

F.S. Now that you've mentioned Unamuno ... What do
you think of him, of Azorín, and of Antonio Machado?

J.L.B. I believe Unamuno is, despite his defects, superior to
the others. As for Azorín, I think his work is absolutely execrable, or only has negative values. He has the virtue of not having
committed certain errors, of having avoided that Spanish bom-

bast . . . But after all, this is a virtue of omission, we might say. And I don't think there is any positive value in his work.

F.S. One could almost say he's no more than a journalist?

J.L.B. Yes, but one would hope a journalist would be more entertaining than Azorín. So I don't know whether he would have been successful as a newspaperman; his articles might possibly have been rejected. He was a person who seemed greatly interested in petty details: the fact of whether it's raining or not raining, etc. Now, as for Antonio Machado, of course he's written some splendid pages but, at the same time, he's written others in which you can see the Andalusian trying to be a Castilian, dropping [Castilian] place names at every turn. Really, I believe I share Cansinos Assens' opinion that Manuel Machado was superior to Antonio [Machado]. Of course, a writer should always be judged by his or her best pages. And I think Manuel's best pages are not inferior to Antonio's best ones. Besides, I think it's quite possible that the fact that Antonio was a Republican and Manuel Machado was a follower of Franco might have had an influence, and I think it absurd to judge a writer by his political opinions.

F.S. Speaking of Andalusians, if García Lorca hadn't been shot, he would be only one year older than you. How do you view that writer who's practically a contemporary of yours?

J.L.B. I've always considered García Lorca to be a second-rate poet. He has always seemed to me merely a picturesque poet, a poet who applied certain procedures taken from the French literature of that time to Andalusian themes. Something like the way Fernán Silva Valdés applied incipient Ultra-ism to certain themes connected with our nostalgia for the Argentina and the Uruguay of old in *Agua del tiempo* (Water of Time). More or less what Güiraldes would later do with *Don Segundo Sombra*. The truth is I have never been able to admire García Lorca very much. Or rather, I think what he was doing in poetry was all right, but that what he's done is not very important; I think it's purely verbal, that you can note a certain deep-seated coldness in everything he writes. As a writer, he's incapable of passion. As for his theater, I don't know whether I can judge it by a play called *Yerma*, a play I couldn't sit through to the end because it bored me so much that I had to leave. I think it was lucky for him he was shot, and I think it adds something, don't you? Maybe in time he might have learned to play other, more interesting games. And I believe my opinion is shared by many people in Spain, especially in Andalusia. I think García Lorca is probably more successful—let's say—in Castile or in Galicia than in Andalusia where people are aware of the falsity of his Andalusianism.[7] And of course, he's probably even more successful in France.

F.S. You once told me that Spain's eighteenth century isn't worth much . . .

J.L.B. More likely I said it isn't worth anything.

F.S. . . . that the nineteenth century is a disgrace . . .

J.L.B. The fact is, it really is a disgrace!

F.S. Okay. As for Spain's twentieth century, I named these writers to see if we could find some major figure to your liking. Juan Ramón Jiménez, perhaps?

J.L.B. Juan Ramón Jiménez wrote well at first, but in the end he became resigned to writing anything at all. The later books of Juan Ramón Jiménez seem as though they were thrown together; it seems as though he wrote anything that came into his head. Or not only any *thing*: any word, any string of phrases that came into his head. In short, I believe contemporary Argentinean literature is richer than contemporary Spanish literature.

F.S. You were a close friend of Alfonso Reyes, weren't you?

J.L.B. Yes. And I believe Alfonso Reyes' prose is far superior to that of any Spanish writer. For one thing, Alfonso Reyes had good taste; he wouldn't have gotten involved in the kind of flashy affectation and pedantry typical of Ortega y Gasset. Alfonso Reyes had a kind of grace, a kind of lightness, a way of saying things as if he weren't conscious of saying them. Then again, we have to remember that Ortega y Gasset was a professor and must have gotten accustomed to telling jokes in order to make a hit with the students, and he would intercalate them later into his works. I have wonderful memories of Alfonso Reyes.[8] I met Reyes when Buenos Aires thought of me as—shall we say—Leonorcita Acevedo's son, Colonel Borges' grandson . . . , who knows what . . . I didn't exist in my own right. And Reyes, I don't know how, saw me as an individual and not as someone's relative. I also recall that Reyes had a gift for coming up with the right quotation for any human situation. For example, we were talking about the Mexican poet, Othón. I knew many of his sonnets by heart; now I remember no more than a single line here or there. And Reyes told me he had met Othón, because he, Othón, used to go to General Reyes' house—General Reyes was Alfonso's father;[9] he got himself killed during that business with Porfirio Díaz. And then, surprised, I asked him: "What? You met Othón?" And Reyes, coming up with the perfect quote—a line of Browning—said: "Ah, did you once see Shelley plain?"[10] meaning "did you get a close look at him?" He'd come up with quotations just like that, on the spur of the moment. Then too, Reyes was an extremely generous man, something I noticed in Ricardo Güiraldes, too. I'd hand in a poem which was a mere rough draft of a rough draft in which I hadn't managed to say anything, and they would figure out what it was I was trying to say, what my inexperience in literature had prevented me from saying. Reyes was very kind to me. He included my book *Cuaderno San Martín* (San Martín Copybook) in his collection Cuadernos del Plata (River Plate Notebooks). He was the Mexican ambassador and, naturally, made friends with well-known authors in each country he went to—he was a friend of Lugones, for instance—but he would also seek out the young fellows who were just beginning to write. And he used to invite me to have dinner with him every Sunday evening at the Mexican Embassy. I recall that I lent Reyes a book by Bertrand Russell on the philosophy of mathematics; I still have the book, with some notation in the margin by Reyes.

F.S. A few minutes ago you spoke to me about a sort of literary perversion that you used to find in the style of some of Góngora's works. I read *Un modelo para la muerte* (A Model for Death) and I don't know who is easier to read: Góngora or Suárez Lynch [pen name of Borges in collaboration with Bioy Casares].

J.L.B. Well, now! I think you're absolutely right. When Bioy and I had finished writing that book, we resolved not to write in that style any more. I told Bioy he shouldn't allow that story to be reprinted because it's a series of jokes about jokes about other jokes, so that we had come to a sort of ridiculous humor.

F.S. I think if you consider the fragments in isolation, the story is very funny, but it's hard to follow the plot.

J.L.B. Still, the plot isn't bad. The trouble is that the plot is sort of buried under so many absurdities. I don't know what happened to us there.

F.S. As I read it, I applauded Dr. Mario Bonfanti's remarks but lost the thread of the plot.

J.L.B. And that's death for a detective novel. Néstor Ibarra told me the same thing: "It's a pity that the two of you write detective stories," he told me, "You ought simply to show these eccentric characters, because people can understand eccentric characters and can even be amused by them, but if in addition to this one has to keep track of a detective-story plot and the solution to the mystery, it gets to be totally impossible; you're writing for two incompatible goals."

F.S. That's what happens to me: I enjoy the jokes but can't follow the plot.

J.L.B. It even happens to me, and I'm the one who wrote it! There are times I don't understand what we've written. That's why I told Bioy it would be better not to have the book reprinted. But he said to me: "Well, someone's going to do it some time, anyway." It's true, but at least they won't do it in our lifetime. I think that reprinting is damaging to us, because I think *Crónicas de Bustos Domecq* (Chronicles of Bustos Domecq) is a good book but that anyone who has read *Un modelo para la muerte* is not ever going to have any desire to read another book by the same author because he's not going to feel like losing himself in those labyrinths of ridiculous remarks, even if those remarks are deliberately ridiculous.

F.S. And that character called Father Gallegani mentioned somewhere in it, is he Father Castellani?[11]

J.L.B. I don't remember him very well. We might possibly have sent him our compliments that way.

F.S. You took a position with that library in Almagro Sur in 1938.[12] Hadn't you ever worked before that date?

J.L.B. Yes. I had worked at various jobs, but not as a librarian. I owe a debt of gratitude to that library because—as is the case in almost every public service organization—there were many employees and very little work. The part that was really work was having to stay in the same place for six hours. But I discovered, in succession, the basement, the roof, some secluded garret . . . , and it was there that I had the opportunity to read Gibbon's entire *History of the Decline and Fall of the Roman Empire*; the works of Léon Bloy; the works of Paul Claudel—these are the writers I remember—which that curious neighborhood library had in their entirety. I imagine I must have been the only one to whom it occurred to read those authors. I must have been there altogether some nine years, and I finally attained a salary of 240 pesos per month.

F.S. Was that a good salary in those days?

J.L.B. No, but as I was also writing a couple of pages for *El Hogar*[13] and they paid me seventy-five pesos a page, it was a salary that was—I won't say magnificent—sufficient.

F.S. I might be wrong but I have the impression that you're not someone who's interested in living in the lap of luxury, anyway.

J.L.B. I detest luxury! But of course, I think the advantages of poverty and indigence have been exaggerated; those of mendicity too . . . Actually, I've had some rather strange jobs. For instance, I ran a magazine for a subway company, and there I wrote, under various pseudonyms, articles on the fourth dimension, on the possibility of reaching the moon, on extrasensory perception, on group theory [in mathematics]; that is to say, the kind of articles an amateur might write on mystical or scientific subjects. I've also written the commentary for an Argentine newsreel. In short, I've worked at some strange jobs, not very remunerative ones, either.

F.S. Why did you leave the Almagro library?

J.L.B. When Perón rose to power, I was appointed inspector for the sale of poultry at the markets. Then I realized that this was a way of letting me know that I had best get out. I went to see a friend of mine in the Municipal Government; I asked him why they had decided that I, a writer, was worthy of filling that position, and he said: "Were you on the side of the Allies during the War?" "Yes, naturally," I answered. "Well," he said, "then what do you expect?" So I sent in my resignation that very day—they had already telephoned to ask if I had resigned. And it was the best thing that could have happened to me, because I was asked to give lectures at the Colegio Libre de Estudios Superiores (Free School of Higher Studies),[14] and later I was offered a professorship in English literature at the Argentine Association of English Culture (from that time on, I've continued, not to teach under that same professorship, but to give lectures on related subjects; I now hold a seminar there on Anglo-Saxon poetry on Saturdays). And then I began to take trips through the provinces, to deliver lectures on various topics in Argentinean as well as foreign literatures. I recall a lecture on the Kabbalah which I gave at the invitation of a Jewish society in Santiago del Estero. I remember many lectures on Lugones, on gaucho poetry, on Ascasubi, Estanislao del

Campo, Eduardo Gutiérrez, Hernández . . . , and many other ones. So I almost ought to join the Peronist Party, because if it hadn't been for the fact that they threw me out of the library, I might possibly have remained a librarian until my retirement, and I wouldn't have had the opportunity to become acquainted with one of the joys left to me: teaching college. I really enjoy teaching, especially because I learn as I teach. This is so much the case that now—I think we've already talked about this— every Sunday a very small group of us devote ourselves to the study of Old Scandinavian. Every Saturday I hold my "Readings in Old English Poetry" at the Argentine Association of English Culture. And I owe all that somehow to the fortuitous circumstance of being thrown out of that library, and then having to earn my livelihood in one way or another.

F.S. In 1942 the magazine *Sur* dedicated an issue to you in amends for your not having been awarded the National Prize for Literature. Who were those judges and who received the Prize?

J.L.B. The first prize was given to a novelist, Eduardo Acevedo Díaz; however, I don't recollect who the judges were.[15] And I think they might have been right to give the prize to Acevedo Díaz and not to me.[16] But my friends didn't see it that way. Victoria Ocampo—Victoria Ocampo, who has always been very generous with me—didn't say a word to me to indicate that the consolation issue was in preparation. So I received my copy of *Sur* and was astonished when I saw it. I especially remember the articles contributed by Eduardo Mallea, by Carlos Alberto Erro, by Ernesto Sábato, by Silvina Ocampo, by Adolfo Bioy Casares, I don't know whether by Martínez Estrada, I believe by Amado Alonso . . .[17]

F.S. When did you meet Ernesto Sábato?

J.L.B. I met Ernesto Sábato precisely as a result of that compensatory issue in which he wrote a very generous page about me. And then Bioy Casares met him. He told me he had "met a very intelligent fellow, a student at La Plata," and we had dinner together one night. Since that time we've been—I believe—friends essentially, despite our having moved somewhat apart superficially, never because of personal reasons but because of political ones.[18]

F.S. Have you read the dedication Sábato wrote for you in his book on the tango entitled *Tango*?[19]

J.L.B. Yes, he dealt very generously with me . . . But I don't know why he quoted such a strange remark in that book . . . , so strange that it disconcerted me. It sounds as though it were written by someone who had never heard a tango in his life. It goes like this: "The tango is a sad thought which is danced out."[20] First of all, I don't think music is born of thoughts but of feelings. Next, that idea of "sad" appears to have been written by someone who had never heard a tango because in any event, what they call a tango-milonga has a bold and merry kind of music. And as for the part about dancing, I believe it's aleatory; I believe that if someone is walking down the street and is whistling "El choclo" or "El Marne," we're aware that he's whistling a tango and that he's not dancing it. Now . . . , I don't know where Sábato got that remark.

F.S. It's the definition of the tango given by Discépolo.

J.L.B. Oh, well, that explains everything, since it's Discépolo's! You've unraveled the mystery for me because when I read it I thought: "This remark must have been made by someone who has absolutely nothing to do with the tango."[21]

F.S. Well . . . , actually, it's quite a famous remark . . .

J.L.B. I don't know why.

F.S. And . . . , probably because of the radio . . .

J.L.B. Ha, ha, ha! Well . . . , but anyway, I don't think Discépolo is the inventor of the radio. And above all, that business about "sad" is what seems so strange to me. When I say the tango is merry and that it's usually bold, and tough ("El apache argentino" [The Argentine *apache*], for example), which is incompatible with the idea of sadness, I don't mean that those *compadres* wouldn't have felt sadness; I mean they would have been ashamed to admit it. I mean that no *compadre* would have bemoaned the fact that some woman didn't love him, for example, because that would have been taken as a sign of effeminacy.

F.S. Have you read Sábato's two novels?[22]

J.L.B. Heavens, I don't think so. But I have read a book called *Uno y el universo* (One and the Universe),[23] which I thought was very good.

F.S. But . . . what? *El túnel* (The Tunnel), which was published in 1948 . . . , you didn't read it either?

J.L.B. No, I didn't read it, because at that time my vision was very poor and I preferred reading short stories. Besides, I've never particularly liked reading novels. I think the novel is a genre that may very likely disappear . . .

F.S. But I would imagine that in spite of your loss of sight you'll manage, in one way or another, to go on reading.

J.L.B. The truth is, I do very little reading these days, because I have to write something, and so I devote the free time I have—as an amateur, shall we say—to Germanic studies; I devote it to Anglo-Saxon or to Scandinavian. And some times, in the evening, someone reads to me—this is a kind of shared leisure activity—detective novels—or rather, detective stories, which I like better—which I still find interesting, especially when they're not overly detective-ish, that is, when the characters are more important than the plot, which is always a bit mechanical. But the truth is, I haven't kept up with the latest literature and I haven't read any of Sábato's novels.

F.S. Did you like the detective novels of [Sir Arthur] Conan Doyle?

J.L.B. The truth is, I liked them very much and I think I still do. And I think one could say of Conan Doyle's novels the same thing that could be said of Estanislao del Campo's *Fausto*: more important than the plot—or, in the case of *Fausto*, the parody of the tragedy, let's say, of Dr. Faust or of the opera based on Goethe's work—is the friendship between the two characters. And in the case of *The Sign of the Four*, of *A Study in Scarlet*, of *The Hound of the Baskervilles*, of *The Memoirs of Sherlock Holmes*, of *The Adventures of Sherlock Holmes*, I think that more important than the plots—which are customarily very poor, outside of that of "The Red-Headed League"[24]—is the friendship that exists between Sherlock Holmes and Watson: the fact that friendship is possible between a very intelligent man and a man who is rather a fool; the fact that they are friends nevertheless, and think highly of and understand one another. I think the atmosphere in Conan Doyle's novels (that house on Baker Street, those two gentlemen bachelors who live alone, the arrival of someone with the news of a crime, all that) is more important than the detective plot. Because, naturally, there are authors who are infinitely inferior to Conan Doyle— Van Dine, for example—who have thought up much more ingenious plots and nevertheless are still mediocre. Maybe Conan Doyle understood that his readers were satisfied with the friendship between Watson and Sherlock Holmes.

F.S. And I, with all modesty, would add another of Conan Doyle's virtues: his sense of humor.

J.L.B. I believe so. But Chesterton exaggerated when he said Conan Doyle wrote predominantly for humorous effect. I don't believe that; I believe that while he was writing, he believed in his detective. What's more, I think this has been beneficial for him. If he had planned on making—as Chesterton said—a ridiculous character of Sherlock Holmes, he would have failed. And the fact is, in any event, the public hasn't taken him that way. On the contrary, when I was a boy and read those novels and then when I read them again throughout my life, I always thought of Sherlock Holmes as an admirable character and not, in spite of a certain vanity or a certain pretentiousness, as a ridiculous character. I don't think that was the author's intent and I don't think Sherlock Holmes has been taken as a ridiculous character by the readers. He has been looked upon as a lovable character, and Watson too, and above all, the friendship between the two of them.

F.S. This question is more to satisfy my own curiosity than that of the readers: I'd like to know if you, as a child, read a novel of Conan Doyle's which I liked very much: *The Lost World*.

J.L.B. Yes, at the time I thought it was very good. I recall that plateau in the middle of Brazil . . . It came out in installments in *Sun Magazine*, and I remember the illustrations: there was Professor Challenger . . . and the other characters, whose names I don't remember. And it was in *Sun Magazine* too that I read *The Hound of the Baskervilles*. All those novels were published in installments. I remember having read, in a biography of Oscar Wilde, that a Mr. Lippincott, I believe, was going to start a review entitled *Lippincott's Magazine*. So, he invited two writers to luncheon and proposed that they write installment novels for his magazine. And out of that luncheon came Oscar Wilde's *The Portrait of Dorian Gray* and, I believe, Conan Doyle's *The Sign of the Four*. In addition, Wilde and Conan Doyle were friends and furthermore they were both Irish, although Conan Doyle was born in Edinburgh, in Scotland. It seemed strange to me that he was considered Irish but, irrefutably, I was told: "If a cat were to give birth in an oven, would you call what she gave birth to kittens or bread?" And I think they were right, don't you?

F.S. Yes, but with that cat criterion applied to people, you would be some kind of Anglo-Hispano-Portuguese, and I would be an Italian.

J.L.B. Of course, but I think that criterion is applicable to countries in which there is very little immigration. Over here we must necessarily use a different criterion, and I think this [other] criterion is right for us. Because after all, what does it mean to be Argentinean? It is, first and foremost, an act of faith. Our history is not very ancient, we aren't able to define ourselves on the basis of ethnicity, since each one of us may have a very different lineage . . . So I believe that in countries with heavy immigration—like the Republic of Argentina, the Republic of Uruguay, the United States—the criterion of the *ius soli* is appropriate; on the other hand, in stable, ancient countries, the *ius sanguinis*, the idea that a man belongs to his ancestry and not to his birthplace, is suitable. That is, I think both criteria are justified. And here we must insist on the fact that what is important is that a man feel himself to be Argentinean, and not probe into his origins, because then it would turn out that there are no Argentineans. Because many of the Indians probably came from Chile. What's more, many of us would run the risk of relapsing into being Spaniards, which would represent a way of making a lie out of Argentinean history in its entirety, a history which consists precisely of a desire to cease being Spanish. And other people would belong to different regions of Europe or of Asia. Nevertheless, I believe we are all Argentineans; I believe that it means something to be an Argentinean—although that something is hard to define—and I further believe that all this is going to become more intense as time goes by. Unless the nations resolve to renounce their differences and to form—as Tennyson wished—a universal state. But for the time being, I think that possibility is a bit distant.

F.S. In that struggle in which you and Elías Carpena take up the cudgel on behalf of Estanislao del Campo's "strawberry roan" against so many others who attack it, what weapons do you have?

J.L.B. Carpena's weapons are most likely more effective than mine because he's better acquainted with the subject.[25] To begin with, there's something suspicious, because the first person who became indignant over the strawberry roan was Rafael Hernández,[26] who was José Hernández' brother and didn't want there to be any other gaucho-style poets around. Later, Lugones took it up again, almost with the same words, in *El payador* (The Gaucho Troubador). I've spoken with ranchers in Buenos Aires Province, in Entre Ríos Province, and in the Republic of Uruguay; I must have spoken with a dozen ranchers. A good half of them told me that the strawberry roan is not capable of being a good horse; the other half told me it can be an excellent horse. Consequently, I suspect there is no strict jurisdiction on this. Besides, I think there's a literary reason: Estanislao del Campo is justified. I think the line

En un overo rosao (On a strawberry roan)

in itself obliges one's voice to take on a gaucho intonation, and that is what he intended. I think that if he had used a horse of a different color, who knows if he would have accomplished this. In regard to the other argument that has been employed against Estanislao del Campo, saying he didn't know the gauchos, I think it's totally unlikely. *Fausto* was written about eighteen-sixty-something. At that time, what was hard, whether in this country or in the Republic of Uruguay, what was hard, was not to know gauchos, but to know people who were *not* gauchos. Because the whole nation, outside of a few cities, was a nation of gauchos. My mother, who is ninety-five years old, remembers the ox-drawn carts in Once Square, for example; and she remembers that the city of Buenos Aires ended at Centro América Street, which today is Pueyrredón. Beyond that point were the poorer fringe neighborhoods, vacant lots, local bully boys, and then the country. I recall having seen a ranch in Saavedra, right inside the City. Besides, Estanislao del Campo was a cavalry officer and the cavalry was made up of gauchos. It was impossible not to know the gaucho then; why, there was hardly anything else in the country. As for the little mistakes which have been found in Estanislao del Campo's *Fausto* or in [José Hernández'] *Martín Fierro*, I don't think they're very important. They relate precisely to the fact that anyone who is thoroughly acquainted with a subject doesn't document himself and may make slight errors. For instance, I think of myself as a real Buenos Airean and it wouldn't amaze me in the least to find two streets shown as parallel in some story of mine when in reality they intersect. But I would make that mistake precisely because I feel so comfortable with the subject that I don't verify each and every reference, and I might make an error.

F.S. When your vision was good, didn't you feel attracted to the plastic arts?

J.L.B. There are painters I've admired a great deal: for example, Titian, Rembrandt, Turner, and some German Expressionist painters. But the truth is that I've never felt any great attraction for the plastic arts.

F.S. We have in Sarmiento a very vigorous personality. How do you view him: as a man, as a politician, as a writer?

J.L.B. As all of the above! I believe Sarmiento was the most important man this country has ever produced. I believe he was a man of genius, and I believe that if we had made up our minds that our Argentine classic was *Facundo*, our history would have been different. I believe that apart from literary considerations, it's unfortunate we've chosen *Martín Fierro* as our representative work. Because it couldn't have exerted a good influence on the country. It's a book that's a sort of negation of Argentinean history. I think that in spite of everything, the history of Argentina has somehow been an admirable history. Think of the War of Independence, think of the Indian Campaigns, think of the war against the gauchos—our civil wars, basically—the Brazilian War, the Paraguayan War; think of all that. And then think of how sad it is that our hero is a deserter, a fugitive, a murderer, and a sort of sentimental outlaw. Besides, he probably didn't ever exist. Because I think those people had to have been much tougher than Martín Fierro. I imagine Ascasubi's or Estanislao del Campo's gauchos must be more true to life than Martín Fierro, because they weren't people who felt sorry for themselves as Martín Fierro does. And they weren't the kind of people who would ask for pity, as Martín Fierro does. I believe that although *Martín Fierro* was written in 1872, it somehow foreshadows the worst kind of Argentinean namby-pambyism, the worst kind of Argentinean sentimentality.

F.S. Who selected the drawing of *Alice in Wonderland* that illustrates the cover of *Crónicas de Bustos Domecq*?[27]

J.L.B. I did.

F.S. And what does it symbolize?

J.L.B. I selected it originally motivated by crass commercialism. I thought the illustration was pretty and I thought it had to attract attention. Seen in a shop window, that book just had to attract attention. A cat, in the sky, laughing at a lot of characters made of playing cards, had to seize the reader's attention. At first, we thought of using one of Piranesi's labyrinths, but then, when that drawing was reduced, it turned out there was nothing left but a kind of small arabesque. And later, once I had suggested that drawing and after everyone had agreed, Bioy Casares gave an explanation for it. He said: "That's fine, because this cat kind of turns out to be Bustos Domecq laughing at all the characters in the book." I hadn't thought of that, I was unaware of that fact, but I believe Bioy came up with a good justification for it.

F.S. And what did you mean by that ironic dedication to Picasso, Joyce, and Le Corbusier?

J.L.B. We thought, perhaps mistakenly, that people had paid too much attention to them. So we wrote: "To those three forgotten greats." And this French lady who read the dedication in Bioy Casares' home said: "Yes, it's true: no one remembers Picasso, Joyce, or Le Corbusier any more." So we said "yes," we said she was right naturally.

F.S. The so-called *lost* or *cursed* generation in the United States, which includes Hemingway, Scott Fitzgerald, Faulkner, Steinbeck . . .

J.L.B. Well, I think you're linking some very disparate names.

F.S. They're simply grouped by era.

J.L.B. I realize that, but I mean . . . I think Faulkner was a great tragic novelist. On the other hand, I think Scott Fitzgerald was a second-rate writer.

F.S. And Hemingway?

J.L.B. I can't talk about Hemingway because I've always felt a certain antipathy toward what he's written. That is, I read a book of his—I don't recall which one it was—that I liked, and then, toward the end, I discovered that the character who to me seemed execrable was felt, by the author, to be admirable. Hemingway was a person who was disinterestedly interested in cruelty and brutality, and I think there has to be something evil in that kind of person. And I believe that in the end he himself came to that conclusion; I think he regretted having spent a good part of his life among gangsters or bullfighters or boxers. And I believe that when he committed suicide, it was a sort of judgment he passed on his work. But my friend Norman Thomas di Giovanni tells me I haven't read Hemingway's good stories and that among them are some that Kipling could have approved of. I hope he's right.

F.S. Haven't you read *The Old Man and the Sea*?

J.L.B. No, but I have the impression it's an excellent book, from what I've heard about it, that it's a very fine book, a book about solitary courage.

F.S. How would you explain the difficult universe of Kafka?

J.L.B. I think Kafka, like Henry James, more than anything else felt perplexity, felt that we're living in an inexplicable world. Then too, I think Kafka became tired of the mechanical element in his novels. That is, of the fact that from the very beginning we know that the surveyor won't ever get inside the castle, that the man will be convicted by those inexplicable judges. And the fact that he didn't want to have those books published is proof of this. Besides, Kafka told Max Brod that he hoped to write happier books, that he personally didn't like what he had done. I find a similarity—and I don't know whether it's been pointed out—between the world of Henry James and the world of Kafka. Both were convinced that they were living in a senseless world. Of course, I think Henry James is a much better writer than Kafka because his books aren't written mechanically like those of Kafka. That is, there isn't a plot that develops according to a system that the reader can figure out, but instead he has attempted to make his characters real, although he hasn't always attained that goal. And I prefer Henry James' short stories to Henry James' novels.

F.S. A little while ago you told me the novel was a genre which would finally disappear. Have you felt this way for a long time or did you ever, in your youth, think of writing a novel?

J.L.B. No, I never thought of writing novels. I think if I began to write a novel, I would realize that it's nonsensical and that I wouldn't follow through on it. Possibly this is an excuse dreamed up by my laziness. But I think Conrad and Kipling have demonstrated that a short story—not too short, what we could call, using the English term, a "long short story"—is able to contain everything a novel contains, with less strain on the reader. In the case of what, for me, is one of the greatest novels in the world, *Don Quixote*, I think the reader would be able to do very well without the first part and could rely on the second, because he wouldn't lose anything, since he would find it all in the second part. Juan Ramón Jiménez said he could imagine a *Don Quixote* that would be essentially the same, but in which the episodes would be different, since the episodes are nothing more than vehicles for revealing to us the character of the protagonist, or perhaps of the two protagonists.[28]

F.S. What advantage do you see in the short story over the novel?

J.L.B. The essential advantage I see in it is that the short story can be taken in at a single glance. On the other hand, in the novel the consecutive is more noticeable. And then there's the fact that a work of three hundred pages depends on padding, on pages which are mere nexuses between one part and another. On the other hand, it's possible for everything to be essential, or more or less essential, or—shall we say—appear to be essential, in a short story. I think there are stories of

Kipling's that are as dense as a novel, or of Conrad's too. It's true they're not too short.

F.S. You like Conrad's works very much, don't you?

J.L.B. Yes, I really do like them very much. I find in them that preoccupation of his with the heroic. That theme is an essential theme in Conrad, a theme that constantly turns up, the theme of the man who has committed a cowardly act and who wants to redeem himself from that act of cowardice. Then we have the feeling for the sea, which runs deep in Conrad, although he hadn't been born in England but in Poland. And then there's the fact that I believe in his every word, and at no time do I think he's making it up or that things don't really happen that way. Even in the case of characters who appear for half a page, I believe in them too.

F.S. You very frequently insist that you're lazy . . .

J.L.B. Very lazy!

F.S. . . . but your works include a considerable number of pages.

J.L.B. A writer's work is the product of laziness, you see. A writer's work essentially consists of taking his mind off things, of thinking about something else, of daydreaming, of not being in any hurry to go to sleep but to imagine something . . . And then comes the actual writing, and that's his trade. That is, I don't think the two things are incompatible. Besides, I think that when one is writing something that's more or less good, one doesn't feel it to be a chore; one feels it to be a form of amusement. A form of amusement that doesn't exclude the use of intelligence, just as chess doesn't exclude it, and chess is a game I'm very fond of and would like to know how to play— I've always been a poor chess player.

F.S. Didn't it ever occur to you to write for the theater?

J.L.B. No. Bioy Casares and I have written two screenplays together: "Los orilleros" (People of the Outer Slums) and "El paraíso de los creyentes" (Believers' Paradise). But those screenplays have been—as someone or other put it—"enthusiastically rejected" by those who read them. So we had to publish them in book form. And up to now it seems no one wants to film them.[29] Nevertheless, I think one of them, "Los orilleros," could be very successful, and maybe the other one as well. But I don't know what the matter is that no one . . . Possibly the idea that we're literary men is responsible for our script not being taken seriously, for our being regarded with a certain wariness, and for our being considered intruders, for people thinking that the professionals are the ones who should be doing it, that we don't have any business writing movie scripts. It may possibly be something like that because I sincerely believe they're among the best things we've ever done, and I further believe they would be very, very entertaining for the audience.

seventh
conversation

On the Desert Island, with Bertrand Russell — The Jerusalem
Prize — Two Juvenile Books — Almafuerte — Goethe — Walt
Whitman, León Felipe, and Jorge Luis Borges — The Poet of
Buenos Aires — Toward Great Argentinean Literature — Borges'
Advice — The Random Drift of the Conversation

F.S. From a strictly literary point of view, what is your opinion of the Bible?

J.L.B. I have many diverse opinions, since we're dealing
with—as is indicated by the pluralized name[1]—many diverse
books. Of all of them, those which have impressed me the most
are the book of Job, Ecclesiastes and, obviously, the Gospels.
The absolutely unique idea of giving a sacred character to the
best books of a literature has not been—I believe—studied
with all the attention it deserves. I know of no other people that
has done the same. The result is one of the richest works possessed by man.

F.S. There is a somewhat foolish question customarily
asked of authors. They say that Chesterton was asked what
book he would have selected if he had been banished to a desert
island and that he answered: *The Art of Shipbuilding.* Speaking
seriously, what would you have answered?

J.L.B. Initially, I would try to hedge and opt for the *Encyclopaedia Britannica.* Secondly, since the interrogator would
oblige me to limit myself to a single volume, I would select the
History of Western Philosophy, by Bertrand Russell.

F.S. In your judgment, what is it that's at stake in the Vietnam War?

J.L.B. I can't answer with any authority. If we're dealing with one episode of the war between Western Civilization and Soviet Imperialism, I'd judge that it shouldn't be condemned. But, of course, it's a more complex matter.

F.S. And in the present war between Arabs and Jews?

J.L.B. I believe that this is another episode of that war between what we like to refer to as Democracy and what we like to refer to as Communism. I don't know what the outcome will be. In Israel I was told that if the Jordanians and the Egyptians weren't stirred up by the U. S. S. R., there would be no problem in coming to an understanding.

F.S. What kind of memories do you have of your visit to Israel and of your receiving the Jerusalem Prize?[2]

J.L.B. The same thing that had happened to me at Columbia University and at Oxford University happened to me there.[3] I know myself so little that I viewed all that as an exercise in futility. I thought: "What is all this business of giving me a Ph.D., putting a cap and gown on me, of an Israeli university giving me a prize? All this is quite absurd, quite strange. There's no point in these things happening to me: it's not my style." Nevertheless, when those three moments came along, I was moved to tears. They made an impression on me and I hadn't foreseen that reaction of mine in spite of the fact that the same thing had already happened to me on those other occasions. But all three times my own emotions took me by surprise, which shows that I don't know myself very well or that I haven't analyzed myself sufficiently. Besides, during the solemnities I thought: "How strange that so many people are mistaken." And, at the same time, I felt gratitude and affection for them, because their good will was evident. So that it was a strange sensation: on one hand it was one of emotion and of gratitude; and on the other, of perplexity and confusion caused by the fact that this kind of thing should happen to me.

F.S. What do you suppose the situation of writers in the Soviet Union to be?

J.L.B. The sparse information I have leads me to believe that it's a very sad situation. If I'm not mistaken, not only is their subject matter chosen for them, but they're told how to treat those subjects too. Just yesterday someone was speaking to me about a Russian—Russian, not Jewish—author who had included in the manuscript of a book of his—which he previously had to submit to the authorities—the phrase "the great Jewish people." He was told that this phrase was forbidden but that they would allow him to publish the book if he would delete it. And he said he preferred not to publish the book rather than delete that phrase.

F.S. There are two books whose authors wrote them with children in mind but which perhaps have made more of a hit with adults than with children: *Alice in Wonderland*, by Lewis Carroll, and *Le Petit Prince*, by Antoine de Saint-Exupéry. What does each of them mean to you?

J.L.B. Perhaps I came along too late to like *Le Petit Prince*. I read it when it was published and I didn't think it merited the attention it had received. As far as *Alice in Wonderland* is concerned, I think it's an admirable, and what's more important, lovable, book. Now, I don't know to what extent the author was aware of the nightmarish quality the book has, although it seems impossible for him not to have noticed it. Maybe that nightmarish quality is more intense because of the fact that the author didn't intend to write a nightmare; I believe that he intended to write a fable for children and that something profound, something that went beyond his conscious intentions, brought him, not actually to a nightmare, but certainly to the fringes or imminence of a nightmare, which to me seems typical of that book and of the other book, *Through the Looking-Glass*.

F.S. Several days ago you had spoken at length of a "vast Latin poet," Dante Alighieri. Now I'd be grateful to you if you would speak to me about that "vast Germanic poet," Johann Wolfgang Goethe.

J.L.B. I think that in Goethe's case we must distinguish between his work and the image of that work. I believe, naturally, that *The Divine Comedy* is incommensurably superior to any work of Goethe's. And let it go on record that I have been re-reading the *Roman Elegies* these days, which I think are Goethe's best poems, greatly superior to *Faust*, the plot of which I've never managed to become interested in. But there is, at the same time, the matter of the two images. The image left by Dante is not a lovable image: it seems to be the image of a man who is dominated by his personal circumstances, by his personal passions and, at times, by hatred as well. On the other hand, the image left by Goethe—not in each one of his works, but surely in the totality or the general memory of his works—is an image which is superior to Dante's: the image of equanimity, that of a man without patriotic or racial superstitions, that of a man who is interested in the universe, in very diverse elements of the universe. That being the case, if we accept the foregoing, I believe that the Goethe cult is justifiable since Goethe invites us to take an interest in almost all themes, in all nations, and in all eras without excluding the Orient. As a poet, I believe he is—for example—quite inferior to Heine, and this will be noticed if one compares Goethe's ballads—for example, that one about "The King of Thule"—with any one of Heine's ballads. At times, I have believed Goethe to be a German superstition and I have also thought that nations select their classics as a sort of antitoxin, as a way of correcting their defects. I believe that it is precisely Goethe's patriotic indifference, the fact that he went to greet Napoleon, the fact that he believed—quite erroneously, to my way of thinking—that the German language is the worst material for poetry: all this can serve to counteract that German propensity to self-exaltation.

F.S. Did you get to know Almafuerte personally?

J.L.B. No. But Almafuerte's poetry has impressed me a great deal. I think he has written—perhaps—some of the best and some of the worst poetry in the Spanish language. Furthermore, I believe that in Almafuerte there is something that is very rare here and—maybe—in all other countries: the presence of a unique man. It's a pity that the circumstances of his life didn't permit him to *fulfill* himself, as they say nowadays. One of the literary projects that have been with me forever (and one that I most likely will not carry out) is that of extracting a philosophy from the confused totality of Almafuerte's works. A very personal philosophy, especially ethics, could be extracted from his work. Of course, it would be very easy to find contradictions in that philosophy. Almafuerte himself has written:

> And, as a real genius, contradictory.[4]

Which reminds me of Whitman's:

> I contradict myself. Very well: I contradict myself. I contain or include multitudes.[5]

F.S. Since you did a new Spanish version of Whitman a little while ago . . . Did you feel that León Felipe's old version was very defective?[6]

J.L.B. Yes, and I still feel that it's very defective. I think León Felipe's translation suffers from one essential error. One of the most evident traits of Whitman are those long verses in the style of the Psalms. And León Felipe has cut them down; and he, in order to explain this, said that the short line was typical of the Spanish *coplas*. Of course, he would have to demonstrate that there exists some relationship between Whitman's poetry and the Spanish *coplas*, something that no one has ever even imagined. It seems odd to me to translate it according to that criterion. Besides, León Felipe's verses aren't even good Spanish *coplas*.

F.S. Is there a particular author who interests you among the Argentinean generation of 1880?

J.L.B. No. The truth is that there is absolutely no one.

F.S. Not even Eduardo Wilde?

J.L.B. Yes, he does. I wrote the prologue—very badly, certainly—some time ago for Wilde's *Prometeo & Cía.*[7] But I think that what we admire in Wilde is the fact that he didn't resemble his contemporaries. I think we admire him for being different—a little different—but not for very valuable virtues of his own.

F.S. I understand that you consider Baldomero Fernández Moreno as the archetypical poet of Buenos Aires . . .

J.L.B. Yes. That is my opinion. And the reason is obvious and no doubt has been formulated many times: there is a sort of pre-established harmony—to have recourse to Leibniz' phrase—between the simplicity of Fernández Moreno's verses and the simplicity of the city of Buenos Aires. For instance, when Rafael Obligado—and let the record show that I am not an enemy of Rafael Obligado—writes:

> When the afternoon bows
> sobbing to the west,[8]

we note immediately that there is a difference between the author's style, between that metaphor of the afternoon as a woman who bows and sobs—the verb, no doubt, is excessive—and the pampas around Buenos Aires which he is describing. On the other hand, when Fernández Moreno writes:

> Ochre and opened into ruts, the road
> darkly separates the sowed fields.
> In the distance, the daisylike mill,[9]

we might think we're dealing with a merely visual little poem and that the comparison of the mill wheel with a daisy is not especially worthy of applause. But we also feel that those verses are fitting for the pampas, that those verses go well with the plains of the Province of Buenos Aires. Furthermore, I think there is another aspect of Fernández Moreno which has not been properly evaluated, and it's the fact that he was an admirable erotic poet, and this is usually forgotten. I believe that Fernández Moreno's fame has been prejudiced by the fact that we don't see him as completely Argentinean. We think that although he was born here he was a Spanish poet. In Spain he is considered an Argentinean poet and this has impeded his being as correctly evaluated as he should be. It is, in some way, the case with Groussac. I believe that we all feel, we all know him to be French. He himself felt he was in exile here. And we don't appreciate his work, we don't appreciate his admirable prose. And in France (outside of *Une énigme littéraire* and the *Cahier de sonnets*—which is not of major importance) he is simply unknown.

F.S. Do you perceive symptoms of Argentinean literature's becoming, within not too long a period of time, as important as the older European literatures?

J.L.B. Yes. It's true that there are and there were many sad things in this country. But literarily, we're off to a good start. Think about the fact that the May Revolution—that is to say, our birth—took place in 1810.[10] And by 1811 we already had the first gaucho-style poems of that Montevidean Bartolomé Hidalgo, we had a literary genre—the gaucho-style genre—which afterward would give us Ascasubi, Estanislao del Campo, José Hernández and, in prose, Eduardo Gutiérrez and Ricardo Güiraldes. And let's remember that in 1820 we already had a romantic poet like Juan Crisóstomo Lafinur. Let's remember that Buenos Aires was one of the capitals of Modernism—Mexico City was the other capital—as Max Henríquez Ureña points out in his *Breve historia del modernismo* (Brief History of Modernism). Just think of the stimulus the presence of Buenos Aires, the dialog with Buenos Aires, must have been for the chief poet of that group, Rubén Darío. And let's remember that right now there is a group of important writers and—I don't know if I've already said so—let's remember that we are perhaps the foremost nation of Latin America which is attempting, attempting with felicity, fantastic literature. Let's remember that in almost all of Latin America, literature is nothing more than a political allegation, a pastime concerned with folklore, or a description of the economic circumstances of this or that segment of the population, and that here, in Buenos Aires, we are already imagining and dreaming with complete freedom.

F.S. What advice would you give to a young Argentinean writer?

J.L.B. I would advise him—and in this I'm going to sound very much like a schoolteacher; and the truth is that I am a schoolteacher: at any rate, a college professor—I would advise him, above all, to study the classics. But, here I want to make one reservation: I believe that in our case in particular and—perhaps—in general, what's best is the study of the classics of other languages, since the study of the Spanish classics offers, at first, many dangers. For example, the danger of wanting to use antiquated language, the abuse of archaisms, Sancho Panza's long list of proverbs, etc. Maybe the same can be said of all literatures. It would be well to study the classics in translation, thus we would be able to capture what is substantive and avoid what is accidental. That is to say, I would advise that imaginary young man to study the classics; let him not try to be modern, because he already is; let him not try to be a man of a different epoch, to be a classical writer, because, indubitably, he cannot be this, since he is irreparably a young man of the twentieth century. And then after a time, I would advise him to take up the study of the classics of our language too.

F.S. At this stage of your life, in which you have written practically all of your literary production . . .[11]

J.L.B. No! Let us hope not!

F.S. Let's say then: at this stage, at which you have been writing for fifty years [. . .]

J.L.B. Yes, that's true. But I believe one must not lose hope after fifty years. Besides, one learns by hard knocks, isn't that so? I think I've committed all the literary errors possible and that this fact will allow me to succeed some day.

F.S. Okay, this is the question: To what extent do you consider your work to be a positive contribution to Argentinean literature and to our country?

J.L.B. I believe that in my latest books there is a certain simplicity, a certain deliberate poverty of vocabulary or—I'm not saying this to praise myself—a certain economy of vocabulary which could be beneficial. I believe too that I've contributed to the boom in fantastic literature in this country, a literature which others cultivate now certainly with better luck than I. A book like the *Antología de la literatura fantástica*, which Silvina Ocampo, Adolfo Bioy Casares, and I published, is a book which should not be forgotten in the history of Argentinean literature.[12]

F.S. Did you read *Cien años de soledad* (One Hundred Years of Solitude) by García Márquez?

J.L.B. No, I didn't read it. The thing is, as I depend on other people's eyes, and I have to prepare my classes and I have to write my work—let us call it that—I have little time left for reading.

F.S. The reason I asked you is that since you told me that if your work had some merit it was that of having promoted fantastic literature in this part of America, and since García Márquez' work has quite a few fantastic elements . . .

J.L.B. Oh, yes? Well, I really believe that this *Antología de la literatura fantástica* that I compiled with Silvina Ocampo and Bioy Casares has been beneficial. Although Lugones had already written *Las fuerzas extrañas* (Strange Forces) before . . . But, of course, Lugones immediately desisted in his attempts at fantastic literature: no doubt around 1906 or 1907 there wasn't a favorable atmosphere in Latin America for that kind of literature. The prose written by the Modernists was principally a decorative prose, a prose filled with colors and with metals and with melodious phrases. And when Lugones published a book which now would be called *science-fiction*, it could not have been greatly appreciated at that time. It's true that people read Wells, but I don't know if they viewed him as being important, I don't know if Wells was significant for them. Maybe Poe's work was significant for them, not his tales, in which there is a certain precision and rigidity, but rather the romantic vagueness of Poe's poetry: ravishing women, with mysterious pasts, who live in old castles . . .

F.S. Are you familiar with Marco Denevi's work?

J.L.B. No, but I have the impression that it's excellent. It's one of those convictions one has before reading a book. What does he say in his work?

(Surprised by this unexpected interrogation on the part of his respondent, F.S. improvises a colorless summary of the first work of Denevi's which comes to mind: "El Maestro traicionado" [The Master Betrayed]).[13]

J.L.B. That idea really sounds good. I once had a similar idea: that Jesus, when He said "I know I shall be betrayed," wanted that statement to be interpreted as an order, He wanted to incite someone to betray him, since He needed to be betrayed in order to have the crucifixion fulfilled. And Judas understood it as an order and consequently betrayed Him.

F.S. What image will you leave in the history of literature?

J.L.B. The image that I shall leave when I'm dead—we've already said that this is part of a poet's works—and maybe the most important—I don't know exactly what it will be, I don't know if I'll be viewed with indulgence, with indifference, or with hostility. Of course, that's of little importance to me now; what *does* matter to me is not what I've written but what I am writing and what I'm going to write. And I think this is how every writer feels. Alfonso Reyes said that one published what he had written in order to avoid spending his life correcting it: one publishes a book in order to leave it behind, one publishes a book in order to forget it.[14] And as far as I'm concerned—

this is something I've been able to verify especially in Texas and in New England—there are many people who are much better acquainted with what I've written than I am. At times they've asked me questions which have completely perplexed me. They've spoken to me concerning the character of such-and-such a personage. I'd ask what personage they were talking about, and it would turn out that it was a character in a story of mine and I had forgotten him altogether without ever intending to. And I could add that I'm like Enrique Banchs; that is to say, I'm afraid that at any moment people may realize that they've devoted an excessive amount of attention to me and then they'll consider me a bungler or a charlatan or, perhaps, both at the same time.

F.S. As a parting question, what is your opinion of the work we've just carried out?

J.L.B. At any rate it's pleasant for the writer and besides, it obliges him to think about topics which he would not otherwise consider.

F.S. And the fact that the questions are as diverse as they are disordered doesn't make you uncomfortable?

J.L.B. No, on the contrary: I think it's suitable for them to be that way. In fact, there is a special charm to the miscellaneous, the same charm that one finds in encyclopedias, for example, or in the *treasuries of diverse readings*, as they used to say.

F.S. Nevertheless, you must have been obliged to put forth a certain amount of effort by the fact that we jumped, you might say, from Cervantes to Vietnam or from the Middle East war to Goethe.

J.L.B. Yes, if I had fulfilled my obligations conscientiously, it would certainly have been an effort, but since I allowed myself to go along with the drift of the conversation, there was a definite pleasure in it, don't you think?

A listing of the literary, political, and music personalities mentioned by Jorge Luis Borges during the conversations.

Acevedo Díaz, Eduardo (1882–1959). Argentina. Son of the Uruguayan novelist of the same name (1851–1921). His now forgotten novel, *Cancha larga*, was awarded the Primer Premio Nacional de Literatura (First National Prize in Literature) in 1942, a competition in which Borges had presented *El jardín de senderos que se bifurcan* (The Garden of Forking Paths). This curious episode is discussed in the Sixth Conversation.

Alem, Leandro N. (1842–1896). Argentinean politician, founder of the Unión Cívica Radical, a populist political party.

Almafuerte. Pseudonym of the Argentinean poet, Pedro B. Palacios (1854–1917).

Alonso, Amado (1896–1952). Literary critic, philologist, literary essayist, college professor. Born in Spain and transplanted first in Argentina and finally in the United States. He taught at the University of Buenos Aires and at Harvard University.

Alonso, Dámaso (1898–1990). Spain. Poet and literary critic. Author of valuable books of essays, such as *Poesía española* and *Góngora y el "Polifemo."*

Álvarez de Toledo, Letizia. Friend of Jorge Luis Borges.

Amorim, Enrique (1900–1960). Born in Salto, Uruguay, he was sent to Argentina at the age of seventeen to attend school. Therefore, belongs to Argentinean literature as much as to Uruguayan letters. Novelist of both the city and the country as well as a shrewd observer of society, his success is based on gauchos becoming fulfilled in their new position as civilized farmers.

Anderson Imbert, Enrique (1910–2000). Argentina. Short story writer, novelist, essayist, professor at the University of Michigan, and at Harvard, where the Chair of Spanish-American Literature was created for him. He is the author of the widely disseminated *Historia de la literatura hispanoamericana*.

The Archpriest of Hita (*el Arcipreste de Hita*). See: Ruiz, Juan.

Arlt, Roberto (1900–1942). Argentina. Novelist and short story writer as well as dramatist. Harsh social commentator on Buenos Aires.

Arolas, Eduardo (1892–1924). Argentina. Famous musician and composer of tangos, such as "El Marne" (1918).

Aróztegui, Manuel (1888–1938). Born in Montevideo, Uruguay, lived most of his life in Buenos Aires. Musician and composer of tangos, such as "El apache argentino" (1913).

Ascasubi, Hilario (1807–1875). He used the pseudonym Aniceto el Gallo (Aniceto the Rooster). Argentinean gaucho-style poet. Romantic satirical poet of anti-Rosas group. His most important book is *Santos Vega o Los mellizos de "La Flor"* (1872).

Azorín. Pseudonym of José Martínez Ruiz (1873–1967). Spain. Nucleus of the Spanish "Generation of '98," along with Baroja and Ramiro de Maeztu. Sensitive and intellectual, he wrote memoirs, short stories, plays, and essays on literary criticism as well as the regions and cities of Spain.

Banchs, Enrique (1888–1968). A fine Argentinean poet noted for his simplicity, sincerity, and use of popular forms.

Basso, José (1919–1993). Pianist and composer of tangos.

Bernárdez, Francisco Luis (1900–1978). Argentinean poet. Lyric poetry with undercurrent of Christian humility. Subjects: children, faith, Argentine flag.

Bioy Casares, Adolfo (1914–1999). One of the most important Argentinean writers of the 20th century. Novel, short story, psychological, rather than magical, fantasy. Collaborated with Borges under various pseudonyms. See: Suárez Lynch, B., and Bustos Domecq, H.

Bombal, Susana (1902–1990). Argentinean writer and friend of Borges.

Borges, Norah (1901–1998). Well-known painter. Sister of Jorge Luis.

Brandán Caraffa, Alfredo (1898–1978). Argentinean poet who, along with Borges, Güiraldes, and Rojas Paz, was one of the founders of the magazine *Proa* (second series) in 1924.

Bullrich Palenque, Silvina (1915–1990). Popular Argentinean novelist. With Borges, published an anthology of writings on the *compadrito* of the Buenos Aires outskirts in 1945.

Bustos Domecq, H. One of the pseudonyms used by Borges and Bioy Casares in collaboration. Combination of ancestral names of Borges and Bioy Casares. See: Suárez Lynch, B.

Calderón de la Barca, Pedro (1600–1681). Last of the great Spanish dramatists. Systematized ideology, theology and basic sentiments of the Golden Age in his theater. Prolific playwright, best known for *La vida es sueño* (Life Is a Dream) the theme of which is the mastering of passions in order to attain salvation. His plays expound Roman Catholic doctrine.

Campo, Estanislao del (1834–1880). Considered the best gaucho-style poet after José Hernández. A cultured city dweller who wrote satirical poetry in the gaucho style under the pseudonym of Anastasio el Pollo. Author of the witty *Fausto* (1866), a comical parody of Charles Gounod's opera, in turn based on Goethe's tragedy. Estanislao del Campo was a great admirer of Hilario Ascasubi, a.k.a. Aniceto el Gallo (Aniceto the Rooster); for that reason and to credit Ascasubi as a sort of model or mentor del Campo called himself Anastasio el Pollo (Anastasio the Chicken).

Cancela, Arturo (1892–1957). Argentinean short story writer and novelist who cultivated humor.

Cansinos Assens, Rafael (1882–1964). Spanish novelist and literary critic who was the leading figure in the Ultraist poetic movement. Finding the name Cansinos in the archives of the Inquisition, he decided he was a Jew; this led him to the study of Hebrew. He wrote a book of psalms (mostly erotic), *El candelabro de los siete brazos* (The Seven-Branched Candelabrum, i. e., The Menorah), published in 1915. He was young Borges' mentor in Spain and had a decided influence on him.

Capdevila, Arturo (1889–1967). Argentinean poet whose poetry, at its best, deals with the mystery of humankind.

Carpena, Elías (1897–1988). Argentinean poet in the popular tradition and short story writer, sketches of manners.

Carriego, Evaristo (1883–1912). Argentinean poet, founder of the poetry dedicated to the humble old neighborhoods of Buenos Aires (in this light, a forerunner of much of Borges' poetry). Borges wrote an entire book devoted to Carriego and Carriego's subject.

Castellani, Leonardo (1899–1981). Jesuit priest and author of detective stories in the style of Chesterton's Father Brown series.

Castro, Américo (1885–1972). Spanish literary critic specializing in the Golden Age. Essays on Spanish history, especially the Middle Ages and the contribution to the modern Spanish character of Christians, Arabs, and Jews. Professor in Madrid and at Princeton University.

Catriel, Cipriano (?–1874). Indian chief of a tribe in Buenos Aires Province. Fought alternately against the whites and against other Indians. Because of treason to his own tribe, he was assassinated by his own men.

Coliqueo, Simón (?–1902). Indian chief of a tribe in the Province of Buenos Aires. He became assimilated to white society and died in bed of natural causes.

Cortázar, Julio (1914–1984). Outstanding novelist and short story writer. This Argentinean writer has been widely translated. His prose contains a wide streak of poetry and hallucinatory effect. Highly experimental literature. Perhaps best known in the U. S. for *Hopscotch* (1963), or *The Winners* (1961). The motion picture "Blow Up" was based on a short story of his.

Cruz, Ernesto de la (1898–1985). Musician and composer of tangos. He, in collaboration with Francisco Alfredo Marino, wrote the music of the tango, "El ciruja" (1926).

Darío, Rubén (1867–1916). Nicaragua. Born with the name Félix Rubén García Sarmiento. Of Spanish-Indian-African extraction, Spanish-America's most cosmopolitan, probably most beloved poet. The most important poet of Modernism (the literary movement that emanated from Spanish-America at the end of the nineteenth century and the beginning of the twentieth). Born in Nicaragua, he lived in Chile, Argentina, and Spain and traveled widely in Europe and North America.

Denevi, Marco (1920–1998). Talented Argentinean short story writer and novelist. Winner of the literary *Premio Life en Español* (Life in Spanish Prize) for his novella *Ceremonia secreta* (Secret Ceremony). Best known for his instant success, *Rosaura a las diez* (Rosa at Ten O'clock).

Díaz, Porfirio (1830–1915). Iron-fisted President of Mexico, 1876–1880 and 1884–1911. Supported by rural aristocrats, the urban middle class, the Church, intellectuals, and foreign economic interests. During his thirty-year reign, there was much suffering among the urban lower classes, the peasants, and the Indians. Opposition to him solidified under Francisco Madero in 1911. Díaz resigned and left for France.

Discépolo, Enrique Santos (1901–1951). Argentinean dramatist, author, and composer. He is considered the creator of the lyrics of the best-known and best-liked tangos of all times.

Eça de Queiroz, José Maria de (1845–1900). Portugal. Most important novelist and short story writer of Portuguese Realism.

Echeverría, Esteban (1805–1851). Argentinean Romantic poet. Author of the excellent narrative "El matadero."

Eichelbaum, Samuel (1894–1967). Argentinean journalist, short story writer, and especially dramatist. He has won many prizes for his theater. His masterpiece, *Pájaro de barro* (1940), has been called one of the "best poetic works of the Argentinean theater." His *Un guapo del 900* is widely known.

Erro, Carlos Alberto (1903–1968). Argentinean essayist and professor.

Felipe, León. See: León Felipe.

Fernández, Macedonio (1874–1952). Author of writings which reflect a unique and somewhat strange sense of humor, he is one of the most peculiar and eccentric figures of Argentinean literature. He is the subject of many witty anecdotes. Open Letter will publish an English translation of his novel *Museo de la Novela de La Eterna* (The Museum of Eterna's Novel) in 2010.

Fernández Moreno, Baldomero (1886–1950). One of the most important Argentinean poets, he practiced medicine until

1924, then began to teach and to write. This post- Modernist's spontaneous, warm, humorous, unadorned poetry of humble daily life won many prizes.

Gálvez, Manuel (1882–1962). Prolific Argentinean novelist. His most famous novel is *La maestra normal* (1914).

García Lorca, Federico (1898–1936). Extraordinary Spanish poet and playwright who blended musicality with plasticity, the real with the unreal, the natural with the stylized, the classical with the romantic, as well as liberal doses of local color, flamenco, symbolism, and surrealism. All these elements combined in García Lorca with a certain grace of form to produce his own unmistakable brand of genius. He was executed by a Francoist firing-squad for nebulous reasons outside of his native Granada, during the Spanish Civil War.

Garcilaso de la Vega. See: Vega, Garcilaso de la.

Gardel, Carlos (1890–1935). Born Charles Romuald Gardès in Toulouse, France, he emigrated to Argentina and changed his name. He was the most famous of all tango singers. Musician and composer too, he wrote numerous highly successful tangos. His death in an airplane accident at Medellín (Colombia) airport lent a legendary touch to his personality which endures to the present day. He starred in several films and is famous throughout the Spanish-speaking world.

Gerchunoff, Alberto (1883–1950). Born in Proskuroff (Odessa), Russia, he is the Argentinean writer (and journalist) who described with poetic grace the life of the Jewish farmers from Eastern Europe who lived in the villages founded by Baron Maurice de Hirsch in Argentina, *Los gauchos judíos* (The Jewish Gauchos). His *El hombre importante* is a satire of a contemporary political boss, Hipólito Yrigoyen.

Girondo, Oliverio (1891–1967). Argentinean poet, married to Norah Lange. Ultraist, aphoristic, metaphoric, Dadaist, surrealist.

Góngora y Argote, Luis de (1561–1627). Spain. Chief of the Culteranist school of poetry. While having produced traditional, popular, straightforward lyric poetry, beginning in 1610 he indulged in a complex, Latinate, baroque poetry which, because of its neologisms and excessive metaphoric language as well as hyperbaton and classical allusions, requires translation into ordinary Spanish to be understood.

González Tuñón, Enrique (1901–1943). Argentinean short story writer. A fervent Communist, he cultivated literature of strong social protest. Brother of Raúl González Tuñón.

González Tuñón, Raúl (1905–1974). Argentinean socialist poet of the Boedo Group. Russian orientation. Brother of Enrique González Tuñón.

Gracián, Baltasar (1601–1658). Spain. Jesuit and moralistic prose writer. He and Quevedo were the two greatest prose writers within Conceptism.

Grondona, Adela. Writer, friend of Borges.

Grondona, Mariana. Writer, friend of Borges.

Groussac, Paul (1848–1929). Born in Toulouse, France, he settled in Argentina in 1866. He was, above all, a severe, mordacious, and ironic critic. As Borges mentions in various places, perhaps most poignantly in his poem "Poema de los dones" (The Gifts), he is like Groussac in that both men were made Director of the National Library and both were blind.

Guido, Beatriz (1925–1988). Popular but mediocre Argentinean novelist, married to Leopoldo Torre Nilsson.

Güiraldes, Ricardo (1886–1927). Argentinean novelist who successfully blended European literary tradition with living native themes in a masterful, universal work. His masterpiece: the nostalgic and evocative novel of the gaucho life that was dying out in his time, *Don Segundo Sombra* (1926).

Gutiérrez, Eduardo (1851–1889). Argentinean novelist who cultivated popular themes. His most famous novel was *Juan Moreira* (1880), on the life of the homonymous malefactor.

Hardoy, Emilio (1911–1992). Contemporary Argentinean politician. Conservative leader.

Henríquez Ureña, Max (1885–1968). Dominican Republic. Fine scholar, intellectual, literary critic. Max and his brother Pedro spring from the most distinguished family of the Dominican Republic.

Henríquez Ureña, Pedro (1884–1946). Dominican Republic. Scholar, intellectual, man of letters, humanist, historian, essayist on culture of Latin America. Lived in Cuba, Mexico, Argentina. Brother of Max Henríquez Ureña.

Hernández, José (1834–1886). Greatest of gaucho-style poets, author of *Martín Fierro* (1872) and its sequel *La vuelta de Martín Fierro* (1879), poems of epic proportions about gaucho life and misfortunes visited upon gauchos by Argentinean Government and civilization and the draft. Written in the style of language common to gaucho in order to have its reading seem natural to gauchos. The poems could be found in the grocery stores of the provinces.

Hernández, Rafael (1840–1903). Argentinean politician, military figure, and journalist. Geographical engineer, Dean of the School of Agronomy and Veterinary, University of La Plata. Brother of José Hernández.

Herrera y Reissig, Julio (1875–1910). Uruguay. Lyric poet of a small select group. He was a link between Modernism and Ultraism.

Hidalgo, Bartolomé (1788–1822). Uruguay. Of humble background, he was the foremost of many gaucho poets of the early nineteenth century. He was the poet of the Independence Movement.

Ibarra, Néstor. Contemporary Argentinean writer.

Illia, Arturo Umberto (1900–1983). Politician of the Unión Cívica Radical, a populist party. He was elected President of Argentina in 1963, and was overthrown by a military coup led by Lieutenant General Juan Carlos Onganía in 1966.

Ingenieros, José (1877–1925). Argentinean essayist whose works were very popular at one time. Author of *El hombre mediocre* (1911).

Irazusta, Julio (1899–1982). Argentinean historian belonging to the Revisionist group.

Isaacs, Jorge (1837–1895). Colombia. Son of an English Jew from Jamaica and the daughter of a Spanish naval officer, he entered politics and held government posts but died in poverty. Poet and the author of *María*, an idyllic, romantic novel with realistic and autobiographical details of the Cauca Valley.

Jaimes Freyre, Ricardo (1868–1933). Bolivia. Modernist poet. Friend of Rubén Darío. Lived in Tucumán and Buenos Aires.

Jauretche, Arturo (1901–1974). Argentinean politician and political essayist.

Jiménez, Juan Ramón (1881–1958). One of the most beloved Spanish poets of the 20th century. On finishing his university studies in Seville, he transferred to Madrid and the South of France, where he spent some time in sanatoriums because of a neurosis that would afflict him during his entire life. In 1936, with the outbreak of the Spanish Civil War, he traveled to the United States. In 1956, two years before his death in Puerto Rico, he was awarded the Nobel Prize for Literature for his more than twenty poetry collections. His best known and most appreciated works are *Platero y yo* (Platero and I) (1942), poetic prose, and the essays *Españoles de tres mundos* (Spaniards of Three Worlds) (1942) and *El modernismo* (*Modernism*) (1963).

John of the Cross, Saint (1542–1591). Spanish mystic poet, his work was religious and esthetic at the same time. He was the last, most intense, most abstract and metaphysical of the great mystics. Canonized in 1726, he has been called the "greatest poet among mystics and greatest mystic among poets." In Spanish, San Juan de la Cruz.

Jurado, Alicia (1922–). Argentinean fiction writer and essayist.

Laferrère, Alfonso de (1893–1978). Writer and journalist of the twentieth century.

Lafinur, Juan Crisóstomo (1797–1824). Argentinean pre-romantic poet of little importance. The Lafinur family, in Uruguay and Argentina, is related to Borges.

Lange, Norah (1906–1972). Argentinean poet and novelist. Wife of Oliverio Girondo.

Laprida, Francisco Narciso de (1780–1829). Argentinean politician, he presided over the Congress of Tucumán which declared Argentinean independence in 1816. Killed in a civil war battle.

Larreta, Enrique (1875–1961). Of a wealthy family, he lived abroad much of his life and was the Minister Plenipotentiary of Argentina to France for a year. An admirer of Spain and Hispanic tradition, he won immediate fame for *La gloria de don Ramiro* (1908), a well-documented and researched novel reconstructing the Spain of Philip II. This novel is considered one of the best historical novels in Spanish and is a well written piece of literary impressionism. His only other important work, *Zogoibi* (1926), attempts to depict life on the Argentine pampas; however, it rings hollow.

León, Fray Luis de (1527–1591). Spanish mystic poet of great intellectual gifts in whom humanism and religion, esthetics and morals all blend in an outstanding poetic sensibility. The traditions of medieval Christianity, of Castile, of the Hebrew Bible, and of classical antiquity unite in his work. Imprisoned by the Inquisition seven years for "Judaizing," his original poems were less than forty; the rest of his poetry is composed of translations of fragments of the Old Testament, of classical Roman poets, and of some sonnets and songs of Petrarch and Bembo. Fray Luis de León has been considered a great humanist and the highest expression of the Spanish Renaissance.

León Felipe (León Felipe Camino) (1884–1968). Post-modernist Spanish poet with moralistic tendencies. An actor in Spain, pharmacist in Africa, and professor in the New World. Influenced by Cervantes, Antonio Machado, Unamuno, Walt Whitman, and prophets of the Bible. Uprooted by the Spanish Civil War, he dwells on the problems and reminiscences of his homeland. Translated Walt Whitman's "Song of Myself" into Spanish.

Leumann, Carlos Alberto (1882–1952). Argentinean novelist and essayist.

Lonardi, Eduardo (1896–1956). Argentinean army general. Leader of the revolution which overthew Perón in 1955. President of the Nation (acting) from September through November 1955.

López, Vicente Fidel (1815–1903). Historian. Author of the celebrated *Historia de la República Argentina* which is not overly accurate but makes interesting reading.

López Jordán, Ricardo (1822–1889). Argentinean military figure, leader of the revolutionaries from Entre Ríos Province who assassinated President Urquiza. López Jordan was assassinated.

López Merino, Francisco (1904–1928). Argentinean poet, friend of Borges.

Lugones, Leopoldo (1874–1938). Most important Argentinean modernist, was a close friend of Rubén Darío. He once expressed a dislike for Spain, a liking for France and the United States, and praised Pan Americanism. His ideology constantly shifted: socialism, extreme nationalism, romanticism, realism, militarism. A fine poet, literary critic, and short-story writer.

Lugones, Santiago M. Scholar of Gaucho-style literature.

Lusarreta, Pilar de (1907–1967). Argentinean short-story writer and novelist. She and Arturo Cancela wrote "El destino es chambón," mentioned by Borges in the "Fourth Conversation" as being written by Arturo Cancela.

Lussich, Antonio (1848–1928). Uruguayan gaucho-style poet.

Lynch, Marta (1924–1985). Argentinean novelist.

Machado, Antonio (1875–1939). Spanish poet born in Seville, deeply affected by the countryside of his adopted Castile. Lyrical, delicate, and profoundly spiritual. Brother of Manuel Machado.

Machado, Manuel (1874–1947). Spanish poet born in Seville. Descriptive poet, influenced by French Parnassians and symbolists. Modernist poet. Brother of Antonio Machado.

Mallea, Eduardo (1903–1982). Excellent Argentinean novelist. His main preoccupation is the isolation of the individual in the modern world, man's inability to communicate and rootlessness. He is best at presenting the individual character within the predicament of modern civilization and in creating "emotional climates." Of his many novels, *La bahía de silencio* (1940) was translated into English and favorably reviewed in the United States.

Manrique, Jorge (1440?–1479). Professional soldier and Spanish nobleman, his fame is due to the "Coplas por la muerte de su padre," the poem he composed on the death of his father, Maestre don Rodrigo Manrique. The work is a sincere, moving, simple but majestic elegy exhibiting filial devotion, religious faith, and emotion caused by the fleetingness of time.

Manzi, Homero (1907–1951). Argentinean poet and composer of tango lyrics. His prestige in this field is only surpassed by that of Discépolo.

Marambio Catán, Juan Carlos (1895–1973). Tango composer and singer.

Marechal, Leopoldo (1900–1970). Argentinean poet and novelist. Author of the famous novel *Adán Buenosayres* (1948).

Mariani, Roberto (1892–1946). Argentinean short-story writer and novelist, interested in social questions.

Marino, Francisco Alfredo (1904–1973). Composer of tango lyrics, he wrote "El ciruja," Lunfardo tango *par excellence*.

Mármol, José (1817–1871). Romantic poet and novelist. Author of the first Argentinean novel, *Amalia* (1855).

Martínez Estrada, Ezequiel (1895–1964). Argentinean poet, short-story writer, and essayist. He was greatly preoccupied with socio-political problems and with the destiny of Argentina.

Mastronardi, Carlos (1901–1976). Argentinean poet, close friend of Borges.

Matos Rodríguez, Gerardo (1897–1948). Uruguayan musician and tango composer. Author of the world-famous tango "La cumparsita" (1917).

Mendizábal, Rosendo (1868–1913). Argentinean musician and tango composer, author of "El entrerriano" (1897).

Mitre, Bartolomé (1821–1906). Argentinean politician and historian, author of two biographies of famous Argentineans (Manuel Belgrano and José de San Martín). President of the Nation, 1862–68.

Molinari, Ricardo E. (1898–1996). Contemporary Argentinean poet.

Muchnik, Hugo Santiago (1939–). Argentinean motion picture director.

Mujica Láinez, Manuel (1910–1984). Excellent Argentinean short-story writer and poet.

Muñoz, Carlos Raúl (1898–1950). Argentinean journalist and poet who lent a certain literary air to Lunfardo (Argentinean slang) in his book *La crencha engrasada* (1928). Often used the pseudonym Carlos de la Púa.

Nalé Roxlo, Conrado (1898–1971). Argentinean poet, playwright, and short-story writer with a notable sense of humor.

Obligado, Rafael (1851–1920). Argentinean post-romantic poet. His poetry included glorification of the heroes of Independence, intimate pictures of human affection and nature, and romantic presentations of national folk themes, including "Santos Vega."

Ocampo, Silvina (1903–1994). Poet and short-story writer who cultivates the literature of fantasy. Sister of Victoria Ocampo and wife of Adolfo Bioy Casares. Has collaborated with her husband and Borges on anthologies.

Ocampo, Victoria (1890–1979). Founder of the journal *Sur*, the most influential literary publication in Latin America from the 1920s to the 1940s. Sister of Silvina Ocampo. Has collaborated on anthologies with Borges, Bioy Casares, and Silvina Ocampo.

Olivari, Nicolás (1900–1966). Argentinean poet and short-story writer.

Oribe, Manuel (1792–1857). Uruguayan general, president of Uruguay from 1835 to 1838. Supported by the Argentinean Rosas, he besieged Montevideo from 1842 to 1851.

Othón, Manuel José (1858–1906). Mexican modernist poet.

Palacio, Ernesto (1900–1979). Argentinean poet and revisionist historian.

Palacios, Alfredo (1880–1965). Argentinean politician. Representative and senator for the Socialist Party.

Pereda, José María de (1833–1906). Spanish traditionalist, regionalist novelist.

Pérez Galdós, Benito (1843–1920). The foremost Spanish exponent of Realism and Naturalism, this prolific writer produced seventy-seven novels (eighty-seven volumes) plus twenty-two plays. On a par with Dickens, Balzac, Zola, and Dostoyevsky, he is considered the greatest Spanish novelist after Cervantes.

Perón, Juan Domingo (1895–1974). Argentinean politician and army general. President of Argentina: 1946–1952; 1952–1955; 1973–1974.

Petit de Murat, Ulyses (1907–1983). Argentinean poet and screenwriter.

Peyrou, Manuel (1902–1974). Argentinean short-story writer and novelist. A successful practitioner of the detective genre.

Piana, Sebastián (1903–1994). Argentinean musician and composer, especially of tangos. The tango referred to by Borges

at the beginning of the fifth conversation, "Milonga del 900"
(Borges only mentions the line "the wind of the outer limits"),
was composed by Homero Manzi and Sebastián Piana.

Piazzolla, Ástor (1921–1992). Argentinean musician and composer,
a sort of "revolutionary" and renovator of the tango.

Ponzio, Ernesto (1885–1934). Argentinean musician and composer. Author of the music for the tango "Don Juan" (1905).

Púa, Carlos de la. See: Muñoz, Carlos Raúl.

Quevedo, Francisco de (1580–1645). Important poet, satirist, and
moralist of the Spanish Golden Age. He may be said to symbolize Spain's greatness in its decadence.

Quiñones, Fernando (1930–1998). Contemporary Spanish writer.
Admirer of Borges.

Quiroga, Horacio (1878–1937). Born in Uruguay, he lived in his
adopted Argentina from the age of twenty-two until his death.
His best short stories afford a vivid picture of life in the jungles
of Misiones Province. He is one of the greatest of Latin American short-story writers.

Quiroga, Juan Facundo (1788–1835). Federal warlord of La Rioja
Province, the subject of Sarmiento's book, *Civilización y barbarie* (see Conversation Six, note 1).

Ramos Mejía, José María (1849–1914). Argentinean sociologist
and historian. He wrote *Rosas y su tiempo* (1907) on the dictator Rosas.

Rega Molina, Horacio (1899–1957). Argentinean poet.

Reyes, Alfonso (1889–1959). Mexican poet, literary critic, humanist, scholar, and diplomat. He worked closely with Pedro
Henríquez Ureña for many years in Mexico City and both
established the Ateneo de la Juventud (1910–1940), a gathering place for young intellectuals in Mexico. In Spain he worked
with Menéndez Pidal and became an authority on the Golden
Age of Spain. Soon after his return to Mexico, he was considered the dean of Mexican letters.

Rohde, Jorge Max (1892–1979). Argentinean essayist.

Rojas, Isaac F. (1906–1993). Argentinean admiral who participated
in the Revolution of 1955 which overthrew Perón. He was
Vice-President of Argentina 1955–1958.

Rojas, Ricardo (1882–1957). Argentinean poet, essayist, and—especially—scholar of Argentinean literature.

Rojas Paz, Pablo (1896–1956). Argentinean poet and short-story writer.

Rosas, Juan Manuel de (1793–1877). Leader of the Federals, Governor of Buenos Aires Province 1829–1832 and 1835–1852. Overthrown in 1852 by a revolution led by Urquiza.

Ruiz, Juan, the Archpriest of Hita (1283?–1351?). Spanish author of the unique and extraordinary book entitled the *Libro de Buen Amor* (Book of Good Love). Today it is probably the most popular book of the Spanish Middle Ages. In the introduction, Ruiz explains at length his didactic and moral purpose, yet the book, written in verse, is often humorous and even bawdy, describing the Archpriest's efforts—usually unsuccessful—to seduce various women. (Today, no one takes literally the autobiographical aspects of the work.) This huge work contains, besides the autobiographical novel of adventures in love, a collection of fables and short stories; a paraphrasing of Ovid's *Art of Love*; an imitation—in the episode concerning don Melón and doña Endrina—of the 12th-century Latin comedy, *Pamphilus*; parodies of humorous and allegorical poems; several satires and encomiums as well as poems both religious and profane, both moral and ascetic. These varied elements of the work are united by the overarching idea of contrasting the joys of divine love (good love) with the dangers inherent in earthly love. Ruiz served a long term of imprisonment on the orders of the Archbishop of Toledo, and wrote at least a part of the *Libro de Buen Amor*, if not the entire work, in prison.

Sábato, Ernesto (1911–). Important, although far from prolific, Argentinean novelist and essayist. Intellectual, existentialist.

Saborido, Enrique (1876–1941). Born in Montevideo (Uruguay), he settled in Buenos Aires as a very young child. Musician and composer, he wrote the music of the tango "La morocha."

Sáenz Hayes, Ricardo (1888–1976). Argentinean critic and essayist.

Sarmiento, Domingo Faustino (1811–1888). One of the most prominent Argentinean personalities of all time, he was a writer, politician, educator, and military man. He was President of Argentina from 1868 to 1874. He encouraged European immigration in order to "civilize" the country. He wrote *Facundo*. (See Conversation Six, note 1).

Saslavsky, Luis (1903–1995). Argentinean motion-picture director.

Silva Valdés, Fernán (1887–1975). Uruguayan nativist poet.

Solar, Xul (1887–1963). His own adaptation of Oscar Agustín Alejandro Schultz Solari. Argentinean painter, inventor, mystic, and eccentric. Friend of Borges.

Suárez Lynch, B. One of the pen names used by Borges and Bioy Casares in collaboration. See: Bustos Domecq, H. Both pseudonyms are based on the surnames of Borges' and Bioy Casares' ancestors.

Tiscornia, Eleuterio F. (1879–1945). Scholar of gaucho literature. He has written valuable studies on *Martín Fierro*.

Torre Nilsson, Leopoldo (1924–1978). Argentinean motion-picture director, married to Beatriz Guido.

Troilo, Aníbal (1914–1975). Argentinean musician and composer. One of the major tango writers and composer of the music for the tango "Sur."

Unamuno, Miguel de (1864–1936). One of the guiding lights of the "Generation of '98" in Spain. Deep thinker, philosopher, novelist, short-story writer, literary critic, essayist, dramatist, and poet, his work displays a preoccupation with the destiny of Spain, a tortured desire for salvation and life after death, and concern for the writers of his generation.

Uriburu, José Félix (1868–1932). Argentinean general who overthrew Hipólito Yrigoyen in 1930. President of Argentina 1930–1932.

Urquiza, Justo José de (1801–1870). Governor of Entre Ríos Province, he overthrew Rosas in 1852. Provisional Director of the Argentine Confederation (1852–1854) and President of the Nation (1854–1860).

Vedia, Leonidas de (1901–1975). Argentinean critic and essayist.

Vega, Garcilaso de la (1501–1536). The foremost poet of the Spanish Renaissance. Nobleman, soldier (died in battle), political figure, he was able to naturalize in Spain the new Italian form of poetry modeled on Petrarch, Bembo, Sannazaro, etc. Bucolic and amorous poetry.

Villoldo, Ángel (1861–1919). Argentinean musician, composer, and lyricist. Composer of the music of a great many famous tangos, including "El porteñito" (1903). His best known tango is the celebrated "El choclo" (1903).

Wilde, Eduardo (1844–1913). Argentinean short-story writer. Humorist.

Yrigoyen, Hipólito (1852–1933). Argentinean political figure. He succeeded Alem as head of the Unión Cívica Radical (the populist party). President of Argentina 1916–1922 and 1928–1930. Overthrown by Uriburu.

Zemborain de Torres, Esther (1915–2001). Argentinean writer. Collaborated with Borges on *Introducción a la literatura norteamericana* (1967), translated as *An Introduction to American Literature* (1971).

When Fernando Sorrentino has cited a Spanish source, the translation into English is by Clark M. Zlotchew, unless otherwise noted.

Translator's notes are indicated [CMZ].

Translator's Foreword

1. Ernesto Sábato in *Sur* 94 (July 1942).

2. Donald Yates, "Publicaciones recientes sobre Borges" (Recent Publications on Borges), *Revista Iberoamericana* 100–101 (July–December 1977): 729–30.

3. In English: *Sanitary Centennial and Selected Short Stories*, trans. Thomas C. Meehan (Austin: Univ. of Texas Press, 1988).

4. The literal meaning of *compadre* in Spanish is "co-father"; that is, it is the term employed to express the relationship between a child's father and godfather. In many Hispanic countries the term is loosely and familiarly used to signify "friend," "pal," or "buddy." Perhaps it was overworked in this colloquial sense among those who handled horses and cattle on the outskirts of the city and thus became particularly associated with these men.

This Book

1. Actually, more than forty-eight months; the interviews were carried out in 1972. [CMZ]

2. This applies to the original Spanish edition alone. The notes have been greatly expanded and modified for this English version of the book. Furthermore, an Appendix has been added containing an alphabetical guide to Hispanic personalities mentioned by Borges. [CMZ]

First Conversation

1. The diagram at the top of the next page shows Jorge Luis Borges' family tree.

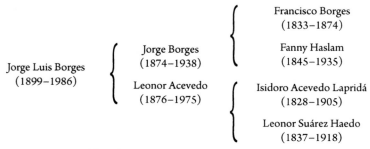

		Francisco Borges (1833–1874)
Jorge Luis Borges (1899–1986)	Jorge Borges (1874–1938)	Fanny Haslam (1845–1935)
	Leonor Acevedo (1876–1975)	Isidoro Acevedo Lapridá (1828–1905)
		Leonor Suárez Haedo (1837–1918)

Jorge Luis Borges' family tree

2. Tucumán 840. This building is now the headquarters of the Young Women's Christian Association (YWCA). A plaque memorializes—incorrectly—Borges' birth in this place. Actually, there are reasons to affirm that Borges was born, not there, but on the plot of land where the building now numbered 830 now stands.

3. The reference is to the building that used to be the headquarters of the Sociedad Argentina de Escritores (SADE) (Argentine Society of Writers), an old, uncomfortable edifice at 524 México Street (on the same block as the National Library) in the San Telmo district, where there still are many nineteenth-century buildings. The façade of Borges' birthplace and of the structure which up to a few years ago housed the Argentine Society of Writers resembled that shown in the drawing below:

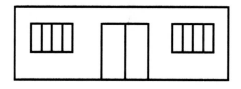

4. The Café La Paloma was a typical saloon at the corner of Santa Fe Avenue and Juan B. Justo, and served as a hangout for underworld characters, neighborhood toughs, and idlers until about 1930. By 1950 it was a respectable establishment with a sidewalk *café*.

5. Actually, and as Miguel de Torre pointed out to me, it is the corner of Juncal and Suipacha.

6. It was not Juan Ramón Jiménez who said this. José Ortega y Gasset wrote: "In principle, it is possible to imagine a *Don Quixote* equal in significance to the genuine article, in which the knight and his servant have other, very different adventures." See *Ideas sobre la novela* in *Meditaciones*

del Quijote e Ideas sobre la novela, 7th ed. (Madrid: Revista de Occidente, Colección El Arquero, 1963), p. 152.

7. "The child learned to read in English and later in Spanish . . ." Alicia Jurado, *Genio y figura de Jorge Luis Borges* (Buenos Aires: Eudeba, 1964), p. 27.

Cf. "Borges learned to read English before he could read Spanish. He first read *Don Quixote* in English translation. From the very beginning the English language was inseparably related to the act of reading." Emir Rodriguez Monegal, *Jorge Luis Borges: A Literary Biography* (New York: E. P. Dutton, 1978), p. 15. [CMZ]

8. Borges describes his grandfather's heroic death in the poem, "Alusión a la muerte del coronel Francisco Borges (1833–74)" (Allusion to the Death of Colonel Francisco Borges [1833–74]), in *El otro, el mismo* (The Other One, The Same One) (Buenos Aires: Emecé, 1969), p. 87.

9. "Historia del guerrero y de la cautiva" (Story of the Warrior and the Captive Maiden).

10. Between 1901 and 1914 Borges lived at 2135 Serrano St., that is, on the northeast side of the street. Today, there is no number 2135 on Serrano; number 2137 comes directly after 2129.

11. Borges was there in the summer of 1934 and, actually, just as he points out, he tends to remember those places in at least four short stories: "Tlön, Uqbar, Orbis Tertius" and "La forma de la espada" (The Shape of the Sword) in *Ficciones* and "El muerto" (The Dead Man) and "La otra muerte" (The Other Death) in *El Aleph* (The Aleph).

12. The issue of *L'Herne* (Paris, 1964) that was dedicated to Borges includes a photograph of the manuscript of his poem, "Rusia" (Russia). So the reader may have an idea of the sentiment as well as the imagistic language Borges used in his early, Ultraist poetry, I have translated the poem [CMZ].

> The forward trench on the steppes is a ship being boarded
> with pennants of hurrahs
> noondays explode in one's eyes
> Beneath banners of silence the multitudes pass by
> and the crucified sun as it sinks in the west
> becomes plural in the shouting of the Kremlin towers.
> The sea will come swimming to those armies
> that will wrap their torsos
> in every field on the continent
> On the savage horn of a rainbow we
> bayonets
> shall cry out their exploits as we bear mornings on our tips.

13. To understand why Borges parenthetically refers to Marechal, one would have to know that before starting to tape, Sorrentino showed him, as an example of the task they were going to perform, the book *Palabras con Leopoldo Marechal* (Words with Leopoldo Marechal) by Alfredo Andrés (Buenos Aires: Editorial Carlos Pérez, 1968).

14. Bulnes 2216, where Borges lived between 1921 and 1923.

15. Ernesto Ponzio (1885–1934) indeed is the author of "Don Juan" (1905). However, "El entrerriano" (1897) is the work of Rosendo Mendizábal (1868–1913).

16. The original poem has some variants with respect to the version that Borges recited by heart. See Marcelo del Mazo, *Los vencidos*, 2d ser. (Buenos Aires: La Editorial Argentina, 1910), p. 139.

17. "If I'm not mistaken, you didn't dislike me, Lugones, and you would have liked to like some of my work. That never happened [. . .]," wrote Borges in "A Leopoldo Lugones," *El hacedor* (Buenos Aires: Emecé, 1960), p. 7.

18. It's worth the trouble to transcribe in its entirety one these "unpardonable impertinences."

(CMZ: I have provided the beginning and the last paragraph to give an idea of Borges' opinion in 1926. The entire quote can be found in the original Spanish in Sorrentino's *Siete conversaciones con Borges* [Buenos Aires: Editorial Losada, 2007], pp. 56–58.)

Leopoldo Lugones, Romancero

Don Leopoldo Lugones shows himself to be very much an almost nobody, a great bungler, full of padding in this book, but that is the least of it. Whether a line of poetry is done well or badly: what does it matter? The best Spanish sonnets have awakened in me a fervor, the ones I've had on my lips in my solitude (that one by Enrique Banchs to the mirror, the *fleeting return* of Juan Ramón Jiménez, and that extremely sorrowful one by Lope [de Vega], about Jesus Christ for whom he spends his winter nights vainly waiting) also suffer from padding. The Parnassians (unskilled carpenters and jewelers, turned into poets) speak of perfect sonnets, but I haven't seen them anywhere. Besides, what is that business about perfection? A circle is perfect form, and after looking at one for a little while, we find it boring. One can asseverate too that with Lugones' system padding is fatal. If a poet uses the endings *ía* or *aba*, there are hundreds of words that offer themselves to him to finish a stanza, and the padding is a shameful padding. On the other hand, if the rime is in *ul* as in Lugones' poetry, he has to make something blue [*azul*] immediately or set up a voyage so that he'd be able to take a steamer trunk [*baúl*] with him, among other indignities. . . .

The *Romancero* is very much [a product] of its author. Don Leopoldo has put out books given over to exercises in ventriloquy and it can be affirmed that no intellectual task is alien to him, except that of invention (there is not one idea of his own; there is not a single landscape in the universe that by the right of conquest is his. He has looked at not one thing with the eyes of eternity). Today, well ensconced in glory and already resting on the obstinate exercise of being a permanent genius, he has tried to speak with his own voice, and we have heard his voice in the *Romancero* and it has spoken to us of trifles. What a disgrace for his fans, what humiliation!

This note appeared in the magazine *Inicial*, under the direction of Homero M. Guglielmini (year II, no. 9 [January 1926]: pp. 207–8). It should be noted, in passing, that Borges is not systematic in his determination to evoke—more or less—the spoken language: he writes *soledá* and *eternidá* [in place of the correct orthography: *soledad* and *eternidad*], but also [the correct orthography] *voluntad; deste libro* [instead of *de este libro*], but also [the correct] *de esas rendijas*.

In 1940 (in his prologue to *Mester de judería* [The Jewish Genre]* by Carlos M. Grünberg) Borges considers meritorious the device that in 1926 he had deemed ridiculous:

Góngora, Quevedo, Torres Villarroel, and Lugones famously have utilized what the last of the four denominates "numerous and varied rhyme"; but they have limited its use to grotesque or satirical compositions. Grünberg, on the other hand, courageously and happily lavishes it on pathos-filled compositions.

Furthermore, we see in Borges' 1926 note he censured Lugones with the phrase: "Lugones does it in all seriousnous."

*CMZ: The title *Mester de judería* is an invented term based on *Mester de clerecía*, which is an archaic term for the type of verse written by members of the clergy, while the term *Mester de juglaría* is an archaic term for minstrelsy. The word *judería* means *Jewry*.

19. See Andrés, *Palabras con Leopoldo Marechal*, pp. 21–23.

20. "To you, Borges, heresiarch of the outer slums of Buenos Aires, Latinist of Lunfardo, sum and substance of infinite hypostatic librarians, rare blend of Asia Minor and the Palermo district, of Chesterton and Car-

riego, of Kafka and Martín Fierro. You, Borges, I see you, above all, as a Great Poet. And then I see you as: arbitrary, brilliant, tender, precise, weak, great, triumphant, daring, timid, a failure, magnificent, wretched, limited, infantile, immortal." Ernesto Sábato in *Sur* 94 (July 1942).

21. In Conrado Nalé Roxlo, *Antología Apócrifa* (Apocryphal Anthology) (Buenos Aires: Emecé Editores, 1952), pp. 97–106.

22. The protagonist of *Martín Fierro* is a *criollo*, native son of the Argentine Pampas, by no means a Calabrian. He is here referred to as "Calabrian" because so much of the first book is a series of complaints about and accusations against the Government and the powerful, recriminations for past wrongs carried out against the protagonist. In Argentina, Calabrians had a reputation for being vengeful (e.g. the *vendetta*), for bearing grudges for a long time. [CMZ]

23. The episode in chapter XI of Book VII ("Viaje a la oscura ciudad de Cacodelphia" [Voyage to the Dark City of Cacodelphia]) is transparent. The astrologer Schultze—Xul Solar—and Adán Buenosayres—Leopoldo Marechal—encounter Luis Pereda in the false Parnassus of the *fauves*:

> The False Euterpe made a sound, a mixture of laughter and throat-clearing. "That's the most noteworthy thing about don Luis," she told me. "He's accused of walking around the various districts of Buenos Aires acting as though he were a tough guy, glancing sideways in every direction like a bully, spitting between his eye teeth and growling the imperfectly learned lyrics of some tango."
>
> "A quirk that doesn't harm anyone," I replied.
>
> "Exactly. The bad part about it is that don Luis has seen fit to bring his mystical-slummy passions into literature, to the extent of making up a false Mythology in which the tough guys of Buenos Aires acquire not only heroic proportions but vague metaphysical contours."
>
> I stonily stared at her. "For that virtue alone," I said to her, "would my worthy comrade Luis Pereda merit Apollo's laurels."
>
> "Your reasons, please?" the False Euterpe demanded.
>
> "Has it not been said that an onerous spirit of foreign imitation has been encumbering our literature? It has been said, don't deny it! And when a man like Pereda goes out and claims the right that the purely native has to rise to the universal level of art, he's ridiculed and reproached to the point of being made to suffer the discomforts of Hell. Well then, Madam, I bow to our champion. And I would reverently tip my hat, if I hadn't lost it in this accursed Helicoid."

"Thanks, people!" Pereda shouted to me, visibly moved. "When I get out of here I'll pay you back with a shot of gin at the pink saloon on the corner. [A reference to the pink saloons frequent in Borges.]

But the False Euterpe insisted. "Let's admit," she said, "that our patient may be a brilliant innovator. Does that fact give him the right to castrate the words of our language and to write *goin'* and *doin'* or *gotcha* and *didja*?"

"A bit of Linguistic mischievousness!" I replied. "The whimsical clipping of an artist. That penchant for castration comes to him from his cattle-raising ancestors."

"All right," allowed the false Muse. "But there are still his neologisms. This gentleman has had the cheek to introduce into the language certain *flagstoneosities, wellwaterisms,* and *bannisterosities* that cry out to heaven."

From Leopoldo Marechal, *Adán Buenosayres* (Buenos Aires: Editorial Sudamericana, 1948).

24. "A un domador de caballos" (To a Bronco Buster) (i.e. To a [Wild] Horse Tamer), in *Poemas australes* (Poems of the Austral Regions), 1938.

25. Manuel Gleizer was the publisher and Francisco Luis Bernárdez and Leopoldo Marechal ran it. Only one issue of *Libra* was ever published (Winter 1929). Alfonso Reyes, Leopoldo Marechal, Macedonio Fernández, Ricardo E. Molinari, and Francisco Luis Bernárdez, among others, were contributors to that lone issue.

26. The low esteem in which Borges held Marechal is also clear in this witticism of Borges':

Un poeta de cuyo nombre no quiero acordarme, Leopoldo Marechal [. . .]

(A poet whose name I do not wish to recall, Leopoldo Marechal [. . .])

From the "Prólogo" to the *Obra crítica* of Pedro Henríquez Ureña (México–Buenos Aires: Fondo de Cultura Económica, 1960).

Nevertheless, this was not the sentiment of the young Borges. His enthusiastic review of Marechal's *Días como flechas* (*Days like Arrows*) (1926) has this ending:

Días como flechas is the most spontaneous May 25th of our [Argentine] poetry: a flag-flying and celebratory book, a book the grandiloquence of which is the accomplice of happiness, never of fear. Die, you sermonizer who brandishes the size of the world to make us feel small: Andrade—Calderón—Victor Hugo!

Leopoldo: Joy which cannot fit into an entire morning, fits into one line of those that you wrote.

From the magazine *Martín Fierro*, 2a época, año III, no. 36 (December 12, 1926): p. 8.

27. From "El ciruja" (1926), music by Ernesto de la Cruz, lyrics by Francisco A. Marino. [FS]

This tango involves a woman who earns her living by picking among the incinerated garbage in search of items which could be sold. For the definitions of the *lunfardo* vocabulary in this tango, see José Gobello, *Vieja y nueva lunfardía* (Old and New Underworld Slang) (Buenos Aires: Editorial Freeland, 1963), p. 28. Also see Francisco García Jiménez, *Así nacieron los tangos* (How the Tango Was Born) (Buenos Aires: Editorial Losada, 1965), pp. 189–92. [CMZ]

28. Borges' predilection for English-language (British and North American) literature is well known. He associated intellectual pursuits with his father's side of the family (including his English grandmother) and, therefore, with the English language. Emir Rodríguez Monegal writes: "Borges learned to read English before he could read Spanish. He first read *Don Quixote* in English translation. From the very beginning the English language was inseparably related to the act of reading" (*Jorge Luis Borges*, 1978, p. 15). [CMZ]

29. Modernism was the first literary movement born in Spanish-America. Developing out of a change in the Romantic taste in the 1880s and taking inspiration in part from the French Parnassians and Symbolists, it influenced the literature, particularly the poetry, of subsequent writers not only in Spanish-America but in Spain as well. [CMZ]

Second Conversation

1. Whereas the tango is well known outside Argentina, the milonga may need explanation. The milonga is a type of folk song which is generally either sententious or merry and which is still popular as an approximate equivalent to country-and-western music in the United States. The name also refers to a folk dance which was popular until 1910. Its essence has been carried over into the tango. Presently, the term milonga is also used to refer to any kind of folk dance analogous to the American square dance and, in slang, simply a dance, a ball. Borges has composed many poems meant to be sung as milongas. [CMZ]

2. Borges mentions that at that time soccer hadn't caught on in Argentina; it was an Englishman's game. See "Historia de Rosendo Juárez" (The Story from Rosendo Juárez) in *El informe de Brodie* (Brodie's Report) (Buenos Aires: Emecé, 1970), p. 40. [FS]

In the Spanish conversation, Sorrentino wrote the name of the game (soccer) with the usual Spanish spelling: *fútbol*. But when he quotes Borges, he spells it "football" to reflect Borges' British pronunciation, as opposed to Sorrentino's (and everyone else's) Spanish pronunciation. [CMZ]

3. The satire of Hitler is *The Great Dictator* (1940), produced and widely popular in the United States. *A King in New York* (1957) was produced in Great Britain. It was highly critical of the U.S. in the McCarthy era. According to Roger Manvell, *Chaplin* (Boston: Little Brown, 1974), p. 216, ". . . the film basically fails to fire because it has been conceived in the spirit of didacticism rather than ironic or satiric comedy." It was never commercially distributed in the U. S. [CMZ]

4. "Inscripción sepulcral" (Tombstone Inscription), in *Fervor de Buenos Aires* (1923).

5. A poem dated 1953. Alastair Reid's English version of it, "A Page to Commemorate Colonel Suárez, Victor at Junín," is in *Jorge Luis Borges, A Personal Anthology*, ed. Anthony Kerrigan (New York: Grove Press, 1967), pp. 24–25. [CMZ]

6. Actually, "Al coronel Francisco Borges" (To Colonel Francisco Borges) is not in his first book, but in his second: *Luna de enfrente* (Moon Across the Way), 1925.

7. See First Conversation, note 8.

8. Norman Thomas di Giovanni.

9. "El espejo de tinta" (The Mirror of Ink), in *Historia Universal de la infamia* (*Universal History of Infamy*), 1935.

10. Raúl González Tuñón, "La rosa blindada" (The Armor-Plated Rose), 1936; "La muerte en Madrid" (Death in Madrid), 1939.

11. Borges makes an interesting slip here. He means to say Baron Maurice de Hirsch (1831–96). Baron de Hirsch was a Jewish magnate and philanthropist who caused the Jewish Colonization Association to be incorporated in London for the purpose of aiding Jews in escaping from the pogroms of Czarist Russia in the last decade of the nineteenth century. He also founded, under the laws of the State of New York, the Baron de Hirsch Fund for the aid of Jewish immigrants from Russia and Romania as well as another fund in the Austrian province of Galicia for the relief of the Jews living there. Through his efforts, six thousand Jews were settled in the Argentine Republic by 1894, half in Buenos Aires and half in agricultural settlements in the Province of Entre Ríos (villages of Moisés Ville, Mau-

ricio, Clara) to the north of the Capital. Apparently, Borges refers to the Baron as *Theodore* (Teodoro) Hirsch because he mentally associates him with Theodore (Benjamin Zeeb) Herzl (1860–1904), the founder of Zionism. In point of fact, although both men were concerned with bringing the Jews out of Europe and settling them elsewhere, Herzl was unable to interest the Baron in his plan for a Jewish Homeland in the Holy Land. [CMZ]

12. In Borges' short story "El indigno" (The Unworthy) in *El informe de Brodie* (Buenos Aires: Emecé, 1970), p. 26, the protagonist, don Santiago Fischbein says: "I don't know if I've already told you I'm from Entre Ríos. I won't say we were Jewish gauchos; there never were Jewish gauchos. We were storekeepers and farmers."

13. In his article "La supersticiosa ética del lector" (The Superstitious Ethics of the Reader), 1930, included in *Discusión* (1932).

14. In the later editions of *Siete conversaciones con Borges*, Sorrentino comments in a note, "Around 1970 I actually came out with such a stupid statement. Luckily for me, I soon modified that foolish opinion, and turned into an assiduous re-reader, not only of *El informe de Brodie*, but of all of Borges' later narrative work." *Siete conversaciones con Borges* (Buenos Aires: Losada, 2007), p. 88.

15. In *El congreso* (The Congress) (Buenos Aires: El Archibrazo Editor, 1971). The English version is in *The Book of Sand* (New York: E. P. Dutton, 1977), pp. 27–49. [FS & CMZ]

16. Juan Crisóstomo Lafinur (San Luis, 1797–Santiago de Chile, 1824) was the great-great-uncle of Borges, since his cousin Carmen Lafinur married Navy Lieutenant Francisco Borges: this native of Portugal, who died in Montevideo in 1837, was the first of that family to settle in the Americas. Lafinur was a poet of very modest merits, and as professor of philosophy, he was Diego Alcorta's (1801–42) professor. Alcorta, in turn, was mentor to those who comprised the Generation of '37, to which Mármol belonged.

With regard to Borges' reference to Lafinur's fondness for brothels, it is heard, in a definitely humorous manner, on the lips of the caricaturesque doña Marcelina (procuress in the habit of quoting from memory from the Neo-Classical theater of Juan Cruz Varela); she makes it known that Lafinur did not pay for services rendered in money (*Amalia*, IV, 7):

> I, my friends, and misfortune make up the three unities of the classical tragedy, as the celebrated poet Lafinur explained to me so many times. He knew that nothing pleased me more than receiving literature lessons.

Two hendecasyllables by Father Francisco de Paula Castañeda (1776–1832) are memorable as well:

Lafinura del siglo diecinueve
es Lafinura del mejor quibebe

CMZ: Impossible to translate, it's a play on words. "Lafinura" adds the letter A to the surname Lafinur, but sounds like the two Spanish words "la finura," which mean "fineness," "excellence," or "courtesy." Therefore, it sounds as though it meant "The excellence of the 19th Century / is the excellence of the best whorehouse (*quibebe*)." But the allusion to Juan Crisóstomo Lafinur is unmistakable.

17. An untranslatable pun has been omitted from the text. The original Spanish is: "Fue en uno de los *almorzáculos*—término inventado por José Ingenieros, jugando con *cenáculo*—de la revista *Nosotros*." The (semi) translation would be: "It was at one of the *almorzáculos*—a term made up by José Ingenieros, playing on the word *cenáculo*—of the *Nosotros* review." The Spanish word *cenáculo* means "cénacle, literary group" or in capital letters, "The Last Supper." In this context, of course, it refers to a literary group; however, the structure of the word is Spanish *cena* ("dinner" or "supper") plus the very Latinate diminutive ending. The non-existent *almorzáculo* invented by José Ingenieros is based on the noun *almuerzo* ("luncheon") or the verb *almorzar* ("to have lunch") plus the Latinate diminutive ending. The point is that this literary group congregated during the mid-day meal rather than at dinner. [CMZ]

18. "El brulote como una de las bellas artes" (Insulting Verse as One of the Fine Arts), an unsigned article in the review *Información literaria* (Year I, no. 3 [1966]: pp. 10–11), attributes to Conrado Nalé Roxlo two "epitaphs." This English translation is provided as an indication of the sentiments expressed and the type of versification employed:

Here lies Jorge Max Rohde.	Yace aquí Jorge Max Rohde.
May he rest in *pax*,	Dejadlo dormir en pax,
for then he won't be	que de este modo no xode
a pain in the axe,	Max.
not Max.	
Here lies Michael Road*	Yace aquí Miguel Camino,
a blameworthy maker of verse	versificador culpable
whom fate turned worse and worse	a quien convirtío el destino
until he became an impassable road.	en camino intransitable.

*I translate the name of Miguel Camino literally in order to preserve the pun on his name: Camino means "road." [CMZ]

Another epitaph (author's name not mentioned) is provided:

Capdevila lies in this spot	Aquí yace bien sepulto
well buried in this ossuary.	Capdevila en este osario.
He was a man, a child, a tot,	Fue niño, joven y adulto,
but never was he necessary.	pero nunca necesario.
His remains should be burned	Sus restos deben quemarse
to avoid any blunder.	para evitar desaciertos.
He died to have earned	Murió para presentarse
a contest Down Under.	en un concurso de muertos.

19. "Today Borges tends to be scornful of the *Martín Fierro* group [. . .]. But [the young] Georgie collaborated actively and generously with the magazine. Twenty-two texts [of Borges], at the least, have been found by bibliophiles. They include poems (three), articles (twelve) and reviews (seven). In addition, he participated anonymously in a popular section entitled 'Parnaso satírico' (Satirical Parnassus) in which the publishers vented their prejudices in versified epitaphs that were comical and at times outrageous." In Emir Rodríguez Monegal, *Borges, una biografía literaria* (Mexico City: Fondo de Cultura Económica, 1987), pp. 175–76. This book contains a great deal of data, but it also abounds in facile generalizations, in journalistic types of conclusions, and in picturesque errors of information.

20. "Nathaniel Hawthorne" (1949), an article included in *Otras inquisiciones* (Other Inquisitions), 1952.

21. In the 1952 edition—besides imagining that Esteban Echeverría was born in 1809 and Lugones in 1869—there is this entry: "Borges (José Luis), Argentinean poet, born 1900, head of the 'Ultraist' school of poetry" (p. 1118). Borges was actually born in 1899.

22. "Aeropuerto: 16.25," in Fernando Quiñones, *Historias de la Argentina* (Buenos Aires: Editorial Jorge Álvarez, 1966), pp. 85–97.

23. Borges spent two periods of his life living at 994 Maipú, Apartment 6-B: first, between 1944 and 1967, and later, between 1970 and 1986. 1967 to 1970 corresponds to his ephemeral marriage to Elsa Astete Millán, during which time he lived at 1377 Belgrano, Apartment 8-A.

Third Conversation

1. Directed by Leopoldo Torre Nilsson. Torre Nilsson himself, Beatriz Guido, Luis Pico Estrada, and Ulyses Petit de Murat collaborated on the screen adaptation of the text.

2. *Poesía gauchesca* (Gaucho-style Poetry), edited, with a prologue, notes, and glossary by Jorge Luis Borges and Adolfo Bioy Casares, two vols. (Mexico City: Fondo de Cultura Económica, 1955).

3. Under the title "Días de odio" (Days of Hatred). Adapted by Torre Nilsson and Jorge Luis Borges. Producer: Armando Bo. Cast: Elisa Christian Galvé, Duilio Marzio, and Nicolás Fregues.

4. "El hombre de la esquina rosada" (literally, "The Man at the Pink Corner"), 1962, directed by René Mugica.

5. Directed by Hugo Santiago [Muchnik] (1969).

Very complete technical notes about these films, based on texts of Borges, can be found in the book by Edgardo Cozarinsky, *Borges y el cine* (Borges and Film) (Buenos Aires: Sur, 1974).

6. "It was agreed that my endeavours [in the plan of the lyrical ballad] should be directed to persons and characters supernatural, or at least romantic; yet so as to transfer from our inward nature a human interest and a semblance of truth sufficient to procure for these shadows of imagination that willing suspension of disbelief for the moment, which constitutes poetic faith." Samuel Taylor Coleridge, in *Biographia literaria or Biographical Sketch of My Literary Life and Opinion*. [CMZ]

7. Gustave Le Bon, *La Psychologie des Foules*, published in Paris in 1895. Current studies in the field of mass psychology generally have some basis in Le Bon and Freud (whose own work on the subject, *Massenpsychologie und Ich-Analyse* [1921] starts with a summary of Le Bon's ideas on the topic). The practical application of *La Psychologie des Foules* in the political manipulation of entire nations is remarkable; it was employed by Mussolini and probably by Hitler. See Clark M. Zlotchew, *Libido into Literature: The "Primera Época" of Benito Pérez Galdós* (San Bernardino, Cal.: The Borgo Press, 1993), pp. 17–18. Also in Zlotchew, "Galdós and Mass Psychology," *Anales Galdosianos*, XII [1977]: 5). [CMZ]

8. In his "Anotación al 23 de agosto de 1944" (Note on August 23, 1944), Borges says that crowded day afforded him "the discovery that it is possible for a collective emotion not to be ignoble," *Otras inquisiciones* (Other Inquisitions) (Buenos Aires: Emecé Editores, 1969), p. 183.

9. Bustos Domecq and Suárez Lynch are pseudonyms used by Borges and Bioy Casares when collaborating on a book; the names stem from the families of both men. [CMZ]

10. "Borges was the founder and publisher of *Los Anales de Buenos Aires* (1946–48), which closed in December of 1948, having published twenty-three issues; the magazine gathered a select group of national and foreign collaborators. In this magazine Borges and Bioy Casares also collaborate under the new pseudonym of B. Lynch Davis." Horacio Jorge Becco,

Jorge Luis Borges: Bibliografía total, 1923–1973 (Buenos Aires: Casa Pardo, 1973), p. 20.

11. It is the first story in *Bestiario* (1951). Later, it was included in the *Antología de la literatura fantástica*, compiled by Borges, Silvina Ocampo, and Adolfo Bioy Casares.

12. Aurora Bernárdez.

13. From "Ultimas tardes," a poem which appeared in *Conocimiento de la noche* (Acquaintance With the Night), 2d. ed. (Buenos Aires: Editorial Raigal, 1953).

14. In *Humoresca* (Buenos Aires: Editorial Babel, 1929), p. 60.

15. The exact title is *Antología poética argentina* (Buenos Aires: Sudamericana, 1941).

16. "[. . .] las límpidas y complejas estrofas de nuestro mejor poeta contemporáneo: Ezequiel Martínez Estrada" ("Prólogo," p. 8). ("The limpid and complex stanzas of our best contemporary poet: Ezequiel Martínez Estrada.")

In those pages, as in so many others of his, we find, disguised as praise, indirect downgrading: "[. . .] the affinities of the vehement psalms of Wally Zenner, of the heraldic forms of Marechal, of Molinari's pleasant chaos, of Bernárdez' Hispanic symmetries " (p. 10). With reference to those "Hispanic symmetries," it would be well to recall "the vain symmetries of Spanish style" to which Borges referred in 1946 ("Nuestro pobre individualismo" [Our Poor Individualism], *Otras inquisiciones*, p. 53).

17. Borges and Pedro Henríquez Ureña compiled a book together, *Antología clásica de la literatura argentina* (Buenos Aires: Kapelusz, n.d. [1937?]). Later (1960), Borges wrote the prologue for the *Obra crítica* [*Work of Criticism*] by Henríquez Ureña (México, Fondo de Cultura Económica).

18. This is an allusion to the opening lines of Cervantes' *Don Quijote de la Mancha*: "In a town in La Mancha whose name I don't wish to recall. . ."

19. Ricardo Rojas.

20. Pedro Henríquez Ureña passed away on May 11, 1946, on the train, in front of Professor Augusto Cortina. Borges wrote a poetic description of this event in "El sueño de Pedro Henríquez Ureña," *El oro de los tigres* (1972):

> Within a few hours, you will rush to the furthest platform at Constitución [Station], to give your class at the Universidad de La Plata. You will board the train, put your briefcase in the rack and will sit in your seat next to the window. Someone, whose

name I don't know but whose face I can see [in my mind's eye],
will say something to you. You won't answer him, because you
will be dead.

21. Borges' quotation of those two lines of poetry in Spanish is accurate:

¡Oh, muerte! ven callada,
como sueles venir en la saeta.

Tercents 61–62 of the "Epístola moral a Fabio" (1607?), an anonymous seventeenth-century poem. The poem has been attributed to various possible poets (Rioja, Caro, Bartolomé de Argensola) and, with greater
plausibility, according to Angel del Río, to Captain Andrés Fernández de
Andrada. See *Historia de la literatura española*, edición revisada, vol. 1
(New York: Holt, Rhinehart and Winston, 1963), p. 409. [CMZ]

22. Mexico City: Fondo de Cultura Económica, 1954.

23. Juan Domingo Perón was Vice-President of Argentina under
President Farrell (General Farrell and Colonel Perón had been part of the
bloodless coup led by the Army to topple the incompetent government of
President Castillo on June 4, 1943). In spite of his "secondary" position in
the Government, Perón actually was the real power. As Minister of War
and Minister of Labor and Welfare (in addition to being Vice-President),
he controlled the Army as well as the work force. Through his control of
the State Radio Station and his oratory he became popular among the
workers. His demagoguery, abuse of power, his admiration of Fascism
led to his being resented by a variety of opponents: land owners, political
bureaucrats, leftist leaders interested in reform, union leaders. Opposition to him reached a peak in October, 1945; President Farrell requested
that he resign from all his official positions. Perón was subsequently
exiled to the tiny island of Martín García. However, one week later he
was addressing a tremendous crowd in Buenos Aires, announcing his
intention of running for President of the Republic. Thousands of people
were brought to the Capital where they were provided with food in downtown Buenos Aires. This unprecedented workers' movement demanded
Perón's freedom, which was granted by President Farrell. This event sym-
bolically marks the beginning of Peronism; it became organized politi-
cally in the Peronist Party (later called the Justice Party). [CMZ]

24. The "Liberating Revolution" which removed Perón from power
and sent him into exile. Perón's power base had been eroding because of
his attacks on the Catholic Church and his unconcern for the Military;
he apparently felt he could depend on his popularity among the workers.

Admiral Isaac F. Rojas took part in this revolution (it was felt that he would not have hesitated to bombard Buenos Aires had it been necessary) and was made Vice-President 1955–58. The leader of the Revolution was General Eduardo Lonardi. [CMZ]

25. At the time of these interviews (1972) the political situation in Argentina was tense and confused. Perón made the most of these circumstances; he was engaged in manipulations which would bring him back from exile in Spain, and have him elected for a third term. He ruled from October 12, 1973 to his death on July 1, 1974. [CMZ]

26. In his youth, Borges' ideas concerning Rosas were very different:

> Nuestro mayor varón sigue siguiendo don Juan Manuel [de Rosas]: gran ejemplar de la fortaleza del individuo, gran certidumbre de saberse vivir [. . .]

> (Our greatest man continues to be don Juan Manuel [de Rosas]: a great example of the fortitude of the individual, a great certitude of knowing he was alive [. . .])

"El tamaño de mi esperanza," *El tamaño de mi esperanza* (Buenos Aires: Proa, 1926), p. 8; cited by Rafael Olea Franco, *El otro Borges. El primer Borges* (The Other Borges. The First Borges) (Mexico-Buenos Aires: El Colegio de México-Fondo de Cultura Económica, 1993), p. 103.

27. The exact quotation is in Borges' prologue to *Recuerdos de provincia* (Buenos Aires: Emecé, 1944): "Montevideo es una miseria, Buenos Aires una aldea, la República Argentina una estancia." (Montevideo is wretched, Buenos Aires a village, the Republic of Argentina a cattle ranch.)

28. The family relationship is, actually, extremely remote: Isidoro Suárez (father of Leonor Suárez Haedo and, therefore, one of Borges' maternal great grandfathers) and Juan Manuel de Rosas were cousins and had, in turn, a great grandfather in common named José Rubio.

29. From the first Argentine Government of May 25, 1810 until the mid-nineteenth century, the former Spanish territories south of Brazil, Paraguay, and Bolivia between the Atlantic Ocean and the Andes Mountains were torn by bloody strife among the warlords (*caudillos*) of the various provinces. In those early days, those in favor of autonomously governed provinces were called Federalists while those desiring one centrally-governed state were referred to as Unitarians. At the time of Juan Manuel de Rosas (1793–1877) these designations were losing their original significance. Rosas, leader of the Federalist Party, Governor of Buenos Aires Province 1829–32 and 1835–52, was defeated at the

hands of Justo José de Urquiza, Governor of Entre Ríos Province; with the exception of the province of the eastern bank of the Uruguay River (today's Republic of Uruguay), which had become independent in 1830, the other provinces were united into the Republic of Argentina under a federal constitution. From Rosas' time on, all that is meant by the terms Federalist and Unitarian is simply "pro-Rosas" and "anti-Rosas" respectively. When Borges refers to his family's being Unitarian he is merely indicating that his family has traditionally been opposed to that dictator. [CMZ]

> 30. All our knowledge brings us nearer to our ignorance,
> All our ignorance brings us nearer to death,
> But nearness to death no nearer to God.
> Where is the Life we have lost in living?
> Where is the wisdom we have lost in knowledge?
> Where is the knowledge we have lost in information?
> The cycles of Heaven in twenty centuries
> Bring us farther from God and nearer to the Dust.

from T. S. Eliot's "The Rock," Chorus I. See *The Complete Poems and Plays* (New York: Harcourt Brace, 1952), p. 96. [CMZ]

31. The precise interpretation of the German is: "The world's history is the world's judgment." (The German for the Last Judgment or Doomsday would be *das Jüngste Gericht* rather than *des Weltgericht.*) The quotation is from Johann Christoph Friedrich von Schiller in *Resignation* (c. 1800). [CMZ]

32. "Nothing fails so much as success." Chesterton.

Of course, all North Americans are familiar with the commonplace "Nothing succeeds like success," expressing the opposite sentiment. Perhaps this indicates a North American respect for success, an attitude Borges here ascribes to the Germans. According to Bartlett, this sentiment is found in an old French proverb and was cited by Alexandre Dumas in *Ange Pitou*, v. I, p. 72 (1854). The only variant of this bit of folk wisdom we have been able to locate is the quip: "Moderation is a fatal thing. Nothing succeeds like excess." Oscar Wilde, *A Woman of No Importance*, III. [CMZ]

Fourth Conversation

1. In the short story, "El otro" (The Other), Borges the young man presents himself to us with a copy of *Los poseídos* (The Possessed) in his hands (*El libro de arena* [The Book of Sand], p. 15):

"The Russian master," he declaimed, "has delved more deeply than anyone into the labyrinths of the Slavic soul."

[. . .]

I asked him [. . .] if he intended to pursue an examination of the entire work.

"The truth is that I don't," he responded with some surprise.

2. German was the fifth language learned by Borges, coming after Spanish, English, French, and Latin. Whereas Spanish and English were learned as a child at home in Buenos Aires, the other three languages were learned while he was living in Switzerland. Borges speaks of reading Heinrich Heine's poetry with the aid of a German-English dictionary and of being able, after a few months, to read it without using the dictionary. See Jorge Luis Borges, "An Autobiographical Essay," in *The Aleph and Other Stories, 1933–1969* (New York: Dutton, 1970), p. 216.

Emir Rodríguez Monegal states: "If Spanish and English had come to Georgie [the young Jorge Luis Borges] naturally, and Latin and French had to be taken as part of the Collège Calvin curriculum, German was the first language he chose to learn." *Jorge Luis Borges: A Literary Biography* (New York: Dutton, 1978), p. 136. [CMZ]

Jorge Oscar Pickenhayn tells us that after translating a book of Heine's poetry with the aid of the German-English dictionary, Borges was able to read, in the original German, Gustav Meyrink's *Der Golem* (the novel based on the Jewish legend) upon which he would later base one of his most famous poems, "El Gólem." See *Borges a través de sus libros* (Buenos Aires: Editorial Plus Ultra, 1979), p. 20. [CMZ]

3. Skimming through the first two pages of the story is enough to reveal a form of language which is totally alien to Borges. A rather rhetorical, somewhat old-fashioned language, reminiscent of nineteenth-century Spanish novels, is what the reader encounters.

4. Franz Kafka, *La metamorfosis*, translation and prologue by Jorge Luis Borges (Buenos Aires: Editorial Losada, 1938). In addition, it contains the following pieces: "La edificación de la muralla china" (The Great Wall of China), "Un artista del hambre" (A Hunger Artist), "Un artista del trapecio" (A Trapeze Artist, known in English as "First Sorrow"), "Una cruza" (A Crossbreed), "El buitre" (The Vulture), "Prometeo" (Prometheus) and "Una confusión cotidiana" (A Common Confusion). The translations of "Un artista del hambre" and "Un artista del trapecio" do not belong to Borges.

5. The actual line is "And marble's language, Latin pure, discreet," from Robert Browning's poem "The Bishop Orders His Tomb at Saint Praxed's Church." [CMZ]

6. The poem in question is "Un lector" (A Reader), in *Elogio de la sombra* (In Praise of Darkness) (Buenos Aires: Emecé, 1969).

7. The trolley actually was the 76. Later, when he lived on Maipú Street, Borges repeated this reading habit on the No. 7: "He waited on a street corner not far from his house, boarded the No. 7 trolley, sat down—resigned to combining the music of words with the rattling of the streetcar—and opened the book, even though the oculist had warned him about the risk to his weakened eyes if he read in a poor light in a moving vehicle." Original Spanish in Miguel de Torre y Borges, *Un día de Jorge Luis Borges* (One Day of Jorge Luis Borges) (Buenos Aires: Edición del autor, 1995), p. 16.

8. John Aitken Carlyle (1801–79).

9. Jacopo Alighieri (c. 1291–1348).

10. In the 1967 edition of *El hacedor* there is a page entitled "In memoriam J. F. K." (The English version of this book is called *Dreamtigers*.) [FS & CMZ]

11. *De la Terre à la Lune* (1865) and *Autour de la Lune* (1870).

12. The Haedos, the Melián Lafinurs: family names of Borges' Uruguayan relatives. He mentions them to show he is not prejudiced against Uruguayans; Horacio Quiroga was a Uruguayan writer. [CMZ]

13. This is an approximate translation of a curious stanza, among so many others, by Herrera y Reissig:

All is posthumous and abstract
and the ideologist spirits
of the Unknowable Abstract
become soaked with monologues.
The stupefied forest burns
in an ecstasy of mourning
and the hirsute labyrinth
of the proscenium becomes electric
with the phosphorescence of the
gloomy genius of the Absolute!

From "Tertulia lunática," *Poesías completas* (Madrid: Aguilar, 1951), pp. 96–97. [CMZ]

14. The line "de los verdes jarrones japonistas" (of the green Japanist vases) is from the poem "El martes, 24 de noviembre" (Tuesday, November 24), while "la vanguardia marina de los cadetes" (the navy vanguard of cadets) is from "Combate naval" (Naval Battle). They appear in Horacio Quiroga, *Los arrecifes de coral* (The Coral Reefs) (Montevideo: Claudio García & Cía. Editores, 1943).

15. I have referred to the influence on Borges' short story, "El indigno," of the chapter "Judas Iscariote" in Arlt's *El juguete rabioso*. See Sorrentino, "Borges y Arlt: las paralelas que se tocan," *Anthropos* magazine, no. 142–43, Barcelona (March-April 1993): pp. 129–34.

16. The story "El destino es chambón" was written by Arturo Cancela in collaboration with Pilar de Lusarreta. It was included in the *Antología de la literature fantástica*, compiled by Borges, Silvina Ocampo, and Adolfo Bioy Casares.

17. Enrique Anderson Imbert has a similar opinion: "The rest [of his works] is an unreadable digression, unless one looks for, among the ruins of that internally shattered prose (that account), the larvae of a surprising, clever, and even poetic solipsism." *Historia de la literatura hispanoamericana* 4th ed., vol. I (Mexico City: Fondo de Cultura Económica, 1962), pp. 415–16.

18. H. Bustos Domecq is one of the pseudonyms used by Borges and Bioy Casares in collaboration. [CMZ]

19. Carlos Argentino Daneri is a fictional character, a pompously wretched poet, in Borges' story "El Aleph" (The Aleph) in the collection of the same name. [CMZ]

20. In "El Aleph." More than once (Roberto Paoli, *Borges. Percorsi di significato* [Messina-Firenze: D'Anna, 1977]; Rodríguez Monegal, *Jorge Luis Borges*, 373–74), parodical identifications have been pointed out (Daneri = Dante Alighieri; Beatriz Viterbo = Beatrice Portinari). In my case, I would merely want to indicate that Borges uses the same phrase (the only difference being a slight change in the order of the words) in two very different contexts: in the article "Encuentro en un sueño" (Encounter in a Dream) (about Dante and Beatriz—*Otras inquisiciones*, 1952) and in the story "El Aleph." The phrase in question is:

a) perdida para siempre Beatriz (for ever lost Beatriz) ("Encuentro en un sueño").

b) Beatriz perdida para siempre (Beatriz lost for ever) ("El Aleph").

It is especially significant that, in the first quotation, Borges refers to the Dantesque Beatrice Portinari, and in the second, to the Borgesian Beatriz Viterbo.

21. It is probable that, even if only partially, Borges might have been inspired by the poet Roberto Godel, for whose *Nacimiento del fuego* (The Birth of Fire) (1932) Borges had written a prologue in such an enigmatic, intricate, and diffuse manner, to such an extent that we can't be sure if his

stated opinions are laudatory or disparaging. See Jorge Luis Borges, *Prólogos* (Buenos Aires: Torres Aguero, 1975), pp. 75–76.

22. These tangos and milongas are on the recording "El tango," on the Polydor label. Edmundo Rivero sings and Luis Medina recites. Side I contains: "El tango"; "Jacinto Chiclana"; "Alguien le dice al tango"; "El títere"; "A don Nicanor Paredes"; "Oda íntima a Buenos Aires." Side II contains: "El hombre de la esquina rosada" (the title of Borges' story which in English is called "Streetcorner Man"), suite for recitation, song, and twelve instruments. Music, concertina, and conducting by Astor Piazzolla.

23. "Milonga de Albornoz," sung by Enrique Dumas, is one of the pieces on the record *Catorce con el tango*. Orchestra conducted by Alberto Di Paulo. Producciones Fermata.

24. "¡Bailáte un tango, Ricardo!" (Dance a Tango, Ricardo!), lyrics by Ulyses Petit de Murat and music by Juan D'Arienzo, sung by Enrique Dumas.

25. "Grab yourself a tango" is the translator's feeble attempt at translating "Mandate un tango." The Spanish expression literally means "order yourself a tango" or "send yourself a tango." The expression is often used instead of "eat" or "drink" to connote that large quantities are involved. The use of the English "grab" as a translation of this Argentine colloquialism is due to its analogous use for food and drink, e. g. "Let's grab a hamburger and a beer," although the idea of huge quantities is missing in English. [CMZ]

Fifth Conversation

1. Strictly speaking:

Sur
Paredón y después

These are lines 9 and 10 of the tango "Sur" (Southside), lyrics by Homero Manzi and music by Aníbal Troilo, 1948. The lines

Me la nombran las estrellas
y el viento del arrabal

are from "Milonga del 900" (Milonga of 1900), lyrics by Homero Manzi and music by Sebastián Piana, 1933.

2. "Alusión a una sombra de mil ochocientos noventa y tantos," *Obra poética 1923–1964* (Buenos Aires: Emecé, 1964), p. 201.

The fifth quartet of "El tango" (p. 174) asks the question:

¿qué oscuros callejones o qué yermo
del otro mundo habitará la dura

sombra de aquel que era una sombra oscura,
Muraña, ese cuchillo de Palermo? [FS]

An English translation of this poem, "Allusion to a Ghost of the Eighteen-Nineties," appears in Jorge Luis Borges, *A Personal Anthology*, ed. and foreword by Anthony Kerrigan (New York: Grove Press, 1967). In Kerrigan's translation, the fifth quartet of "The Tango" (p. 158) is rendered:

What obscure alleyways or wasteland
Of heaven is darkened by the hard
Shade of the man who was shadow,
Muraña, that Knife of Palermo? [CMZ]

In addition, *El informe de Brodie* (Buenos Aires: Emecé, 1970) contains the short story, "Juan Muraña." [FS]

3. "El truco," in *Fervor de Buenos Aires* (1923).

4. *Mate* or *yerba mate*, variously translated as "Paraguay tea" and "Brazilian holly." An infusion of this herb is as popular in Argentina as coffee is in the United States or tea in England or China. In Paraguay, Uruguay, Argentina, and southern Brasil it has traditionally been drunk from a gourd (which has evolved into man-made artifacts in various shapes, e.g. a fish, usually made of silver) by means of a metal, usually silver, tube employed as a straw. [CMZ]

5. All of Canto LV (lines 10,506–10,719) is devoted to *truco*.

6. Arturo Jauretche, *El Paso de los Libres* (Buenos Aires, 1934). The Second Edition of the poem (Buenos Aires: Coyoacán, 1960) has a "Prólogo" by Jorge Abelardo Ramos.

7. In the 1920s and 1930s, the majority of Argentinean writers born around the turn of the century belonged to the Unión Cívica Radical, Yrigoyen's populist-oriented political party. With the passage of time, however, they abandoned the Radical Party in favor of other parties. Raúl González Tuñón became a Communist; Borges, a Conservative; Jauretche and Leopoldo Marechal, Peronists. The Peronism of Jauretche and Marechal no doubt helps to explain Borges' antipathy toward them. In addition to his writing (political treatises, historical and sociological works—nothing literary), Jauretche held a high position during Perón's first term of office: he was President of the Bank of the Province of Buenos Aires. [CMZ]

8. In 1930, General José Félix Uriburu overturned the government of Hipólito Yrigoyen and served as President of the Argentine Nation from 1930 to 1932.

9. "La fundación mítica de Buenos Aires" (The Mythical Founding of Buenos Aires), incorrectly entitled "La fundación mitológica de Buenos

Aires" (The Mythological Founding of Buenos Aires) in the first edition, is a poem which expresses Borges' impressions of his native city as he rediscovers it upon his return from Europe. It is in the collection *Cuaderno San Martín* (San Martín Notebook) (Buenos Aires: Editorial Proa, 1929). The title of the book has no relation to the Argentinean hero of Independence, José San Martín, but is the brand name of the notebook Borges was using to write those poems. See Jorge Luis Borges, "An Autobiographical Essay," in *The Aleph and Other Stories, 1933–1969* (New York: Dutton, 1970), pp. 203–60. [FS & CMZ]

10. Borges refers to the Unión Cívica Radical: a populist party. See note 7 above.

> When Irigoyen began his campaign for a second term as president [1928], Georgie figured prominently as one of his supporters. A now forgotten record, written in 1944 by Ulises Petit de Murat, another member of that group, provides an unexpected vision of Georgie as a political activist. Probably under the influence of Francisco López Merino, a young poet who was their mutual friend, Georgie and Ulises decided to join Irigoyen's supporters. According to Ulises's testimony, they both believed that *el Peludo* (the Hairy One) probably didn't have a chance of being elected, that his enemies would probably rig the election, and since his candidacy seemed a lost cause, they had to devote all their enthusiasm to it. They came up with the idea of forming a Committee of Young Intellectuals, in which they were soon joined by Francisco Luis Bernárdez, Raúl González Tuñón, and Sixto Pondal Ríos. The day on which they visited the central committee in Buenos Aires, they were received by its president, whose speeches bored them to tears. Suddenly, and in the accent of a *compadrito*, Georgie turned to Ulises and said: "Che . . . When are the *empanadas* wrapped in lists of the appointees coming?"

Emir Rodríguez Monegal, *Borges, una biografía literaria* (Mexico City: Fondo de Cultura Económica, 1987), pp. 206–7.

11. Quoting again from Rodríguez Monegal, *Borges, una biografía literaria* (p. 208):

> Georgie's reaction to the coup [of General José Félix Uriburu on September 6, 1930] can be seen in some letters he wrote to Alfonso Reyes, who had been transferred to Rio de Janeiro. When Reyes was the Mexican Ambassador to Argentina, he

made it clear that he was an admirer of Irigoyen. To his anxious questions about what happened to the President, Georgie gave a measured, although quite subjective, response. He referred to Irigoyen as the *Doctor*, which was a way of distancing himself with irony:

> With regard to the *Doctor's* elimination, I can assure you that, discounting the need for it, its final kindness, the justice of it, we are now left with a most unpleasant atmosphere. The revolution (or military takeover supported by the public) is a victory of good sense over ineptitude, over frequent dishonesty and obfuscation, but all these evils being defeated corresponded to a mythology, to affection, to happiness—to the outlandish image of the *Doctor*, silent conspirator in the Casa Rosada [the President's residence] itself—

12. The same sentiment is found in Borges' story, "La forma de la espada" (The Shape of the Sword): "I told him that a gentleman can be interested in lost causes only . . ." Within the conversation with Fernando Sorrentino, Borges uses the Spanish word *caballero*; interestingly, in the Spanish text of "La forma de la espada" it is the English term *gentleman* that is used. This may be because it is a native speaker of English who is talking: the Irishman, Moon. See *Ficciones* (Buenos Aires: Emecé Editores, 1956), p. 121. [CMZ]

13. "A Francisco López Merino," in *Cuaderno San Martín* (1929).

14. 222 Quintana, the house in which they lived from 1924 to 1930. From 1942 to 1944 he lived in an apartment on the other side of the street, 263 Quintana.

15. Francisco López Merino's suicide is brought to mind in "Mayo 20, 1928," a date which contradicts that of May 22, given by Borges in the "Conversación." See *Elogio de la sombra* (In Praise of Darkness) (Buenos Aires: Emecé, 1969).

16. Alicia Jurado's words on the matter: "[The lecture] was read by a friend of his—Manuel Rojas Silveyra—at the Instituto Popular de Conferencias of [the newspaper] *La Prensa*, in 1927; Borges used his poor vision as an excuse for not doing it personally, and listened to it from the audience, on the point of fleeing from moment to moment, as he later confessed." See Alicia Jurado, *Genio y figura de Jorge Luis Borges* (Buenos Aires: Eudeba, 1964), p. 13. [FS]

This fear of public speaking, later overcome by Borges in his need to earn his living by giving lectures and by teaching, after his dismissal from his post as librarian under Perón, is reminiscent of the same type of phobia present in the great Spanish novelist, Benito Pérez Galdós, who more than once had his own speeches read for him. See H. Chonon Berkowitz, *Pérez Galdós: Spanish Liberal Crusader* (Madison: Univ. of Wisconsin Press, 1948), p. 171. [CMZ]

17. Half in jest and half seriously, people were saying that Perón would return from exile in a black airplane to rule once more. [CMZ]

18. Six issues of the *Revista de América* were published (December 1924–July 1926). The board of directors was composed of Carlos A. Erro, Leonidas de Vedia, and Enrique Lavié.

19. This is possibly a reference to "Sonata de soledad" (Sonata of Solitude), the third work in *Cuentos para una inglesa desesperada* (Stories for a Desperate Englishwoman), 1926.

20. "El curioso impertinente" (The Curious Impertinent) is a novel inserted within the novel *Don Quixote* (First Part, Chapters XXXIII–XXXV), 1605. It was later published as an independent book in 1608. Its characteristics are similar to those of Cervantes' *Exemplary Novels* and its plot derives from a story narrated in Canto 43 of Ariosto's *Orlando Furioso* which in turn stems from a folk story of Oriental provenance ("Story of Two Friends"). In "The Curious Impertinent" a recently-married young man prevails upon his best friend to attempt to seduce his young bride in order to test her character; the plan ends in tragedy. [CMZ]

21. The three annotated editions of *Martín Fierro* mentioned by Borges are by: Santiago M. Lugones (Buenos Aires: Centurión, 1926); Eleuterio F. Tiscornia in two volumes (Buenos Aires: Facultad de Filosofía y Letras de la Universidad de Buenos Aires, 1925–30); Carlos Alberto Leumann (Buenos Aires: Estrada, 1945).

22. Directed by Manuel Antín (1969).

Sixth Conversation

1. *Civilización y barbarie: Vida de Juan Facundo Quiroga* (Civilization and Barbarism: The Life of Juan Facundo Quiroga), later re-named *Facundo o Civilización y barbarie* (Facundo or Civilization and Barbarism) but usually referred to simply as *Facundo*, written by Domingo Faustino Sarmiento (see Appendix) in 1845, deals with the life of Juan Facundo Quiroga, warlord of La Rioja Province. The book seeks to equate barbarism with the countryside and the gaucho (like Quiroga and his mounted troops) as opposed to the civilization of the cities. Sarmiento's solution to the problem created by the "barbaric" gauchos is a political program for national reconstruction which includes public education, large-scale

immigration from Europe, and technical progress. Although Facundo is a historical figure, he takes on a larger-than-life appearance in Sarmiento's book because he is the symbol of Barbarism; in this way Borges is justified in saying that Sarmiento "invented Facundo Quiroga—more or less." Still, as fantastic and exaggerated as Facundo may be within the book, he was real, and as cruel and barbaric as Sarmiento presents him. [CMZ]

2. Borges modified the following verses of that poem: line 10, which used to read: "El general Quiroga quiso entrar al infierno" (General Quiroga tried to enter Hell) was changed into "El general Quiroga quiso entrar en la sombra" (General Quiroga tried to enter the shadows) with which he sacrificed the assonant rhyme ABAB of that quartet of the 1925 version.

Line 20, "Pero en llegando al sitio nombrao Barranca Yaco" (But when he came to the place called Barranca Yaco) was replaced by the more readable "Pero al brillar el día sobre Barranca Yaco" (But when daylight shone on Barranca Yaco).

The last stanza of the poem is almost entirely reworked.

3. Alicia Jurado gives 1929 as the date of the Second Municipal Prize for Literature, *Genio y figura de Jorge Luis Borges* (Buenos Aires: Eudeba, 1964), p. 7. The decision was as follows: *Prose*: First Prize—Roberto Gache; Second Prize—Jorge Luis Borges; Third Prize—Enrique González Tuñón. *Poetry*: First Prize—Rafael Jijena Sánchez; Second Prize—Raúl González Tuñón; Third Prize—Miguel Alfredo D'Elía.

4. The Spanish word *más* may be translated as "plus"; the word *y* means "and." The name *Pi* can also stand for the Greek letter *pi*. Therefore, his signature "+ y Π" (plus and pi), pronounced in Spanish, would give his name: Mas y Pi. [CMZ]

5. The 1930 Borges scoffed at Rubén Darío. In 1954 he included the following act of contrition at the bottom of the page: "I hold on to these impertinent remarks in order to punish myself for having written them. In those days I thought Lugones' poetry was superior to Darío's. It is true that I also thought Quevedo's was superior to Góngora's." *Evaristo Carriego* (Buenos Aires: Emecé Editores, 1967), p. 55.

6. Here Borges' judgments are in line with much of Góngora criticism which sees two Góngoras: the early Góngora, popular and musically lyrical; the later Góngora, intricate, false, labyrinthine, even literarily perverted (as Borges says). [CMZ]

However, the great Spanish critic, Dámaso Alonso, has demonstrated that this viewpoint that "the separation of Góngora's literary life into two epochs, one entirely natural and clear and the other tremendously artificial and obscure, is totally false." See Dámaso Alonso, *Góngora y el "Polifemo,"* 4th ed., vol. 1 (Madrid: Gredos, 1961), pp. 84–101. [FS]

7. Castile, Galicia, Andalusia: Spain is composed of many regions which are culturally and linguistically distinct. Castile (Old and New) lies in the geographical center of the Iberian Peninsula and contains the capital city, Madrid. Its language, Castilian, is the official language of Spain and is synonymous with "Spanish." Most of its land ranges from arid to semi-arid and suffers extremes of heat and cold; this fact is partly responsible for the Castilians' conceiving of themselves as a stoical people able to endure hardship.

Galicia is located in the extreme North West of the Peninsula in a humid, temperate, foggy, drizzly region. The Galicians' speech is a dialect of Portuguese rather than Spanish, although most of them are bilingual, speaking Castilian too. The Celtic element is stronger in Galicia than in other regions of Spain and the people, *Gallegos*, are thought of as being dreamy, superstitious, and (like the Portuguese) nostalgic. The medieval center for religious pilgrimages, Santiago de Compostela, is located in this area. Bagpipes are the traditional musical instrument.

Sunny Andalusia is the region that most foreigners think of when they think of Spain. Comprising the Southern Tier of Spain and containing the cities of Seville, Granada (with that monument of Moorish architecture, the Alhambra), Córdoba, Málaga, and Jerez (the last two cities famous for their wines), it is the region of the Iberian Peninsula which lay under Moslem domination the longest. The Arab and Hebrew elements are very strong in Andalusian music (practically synonymous with *flamenco*). The performance of this musical art (instrumental, vocal, dance) is associated with the Gypsies who abound in this region and who have influenced the speech of the non-Gypsies around them. The language spoken in Andalusia is a dialect of Castilian which is considered "non-standard" by other Spaniards; actually, the Spanish of the New World derives from the Andalusian variety of Castilian.

Catalonia, in the Northeastern sector of the Peninsula (it includes the great port of Barcelona), has its own language, Catalán (closely related to the Provençal of Southern France), and is noted for the industrial and commercial talents of its people.

The Basque Provinces of North Central Spain produce expert sheep herders and fishermen as well as bankers and industrialists. The Basque language, which subsists in small, isolated villages, and, since the death of Francisco Franco, is being taught in the schools of this region, is not a Romance language; it is not even a member of the Indo-European family and is related to no other language in the world, although there are some theories that it may be distantly related to some of the languages of the Caucasus region.

The other regions of Spain are Navarra, Aragón, Valencia, Murcia, Asturias, León, and Extremadura. Traditionally, the Spaniard's first allegiance is to his native region, his *patria chica* (small homeland), and only secondarily to Spain. [CMZ]

8. Alfonso Reyes was named Mexican Ambassador in Buenos Aires in 1927.

9. Bernardo Reyes (1850–1913) led an uprising, in which he met his death, against Mexican President Francisco I. Madero.

10. "Ah, did you once see Shelley plain, / And did he stop to speak to you?" in Robert Browning's poem "Memorabilia" contained in his *Lyrics*. [CMZ]

11. *Un modelo para la muerte* (Buenos Aires: Edicom, 1970), p. 72. [FS]

The fictional Father Gallegani's name appears, to the Spanish-speaker, an Italian form of the Spanish word for the inhabitants of Galicia (*gallegos*) in Spain; it is obviously modeled on the name of Father Castellani, an actual person whose Italian surname resembles the Spanish term for the inhabitants of Castile (*castellanos*), another region in Spain. Father Castellani and Borges share a mutual dislike for each other. [CMZ]

12. The Biblioteca Miguel Cané, located at 4319 Carlos Calvo, between Muñiz and La Plata Avenue. It should be noted that, in "El Aleph," the ridiculous Carlos Argentino Daneri "fills who-knows-what subordinate position in an unreadable library on the outskirts of the Southside [of Buenos Aires]" This institution, as we later see, is the Biblioteca Juan Crisóstomo Lafinur. [FS]

Borges was First Assistant at the Miguel Cané municipal library in Almagro Sur. He finally was promoted to Third Official. [CMZ]

13. An excellent selection of these works (October 16, 1936–December 13, 1940) in *Textos cautivos. Ensayos y reseñas en "El Hogar,"* eds. Enrique Sacerio-Garí and Emir Rodríguez Monegal (Barcelona: Tusquets, 1986).

14. His lectures at the Argentine Association of English Culture were to be on British literature, those for the Free School of Higher Studies would concern American letters. He would lecture on Hawthorne, Poe, Thoreau, Emerson, Melville, Whitman, Twain, Henry James, and Veblen. See Borges, "An Autobiographical Essay," in *The Aleph and Other Stories, 1933–1969* (New York: Dutton, 1970), pp. 244–45. [CMZ]

15. "In 1942, Borges presented himself before the Premio Nacional de Literatura (National Prize for Literature) with *Ficciones*. He received no prize; Eduardo Acevedo Díaz and César Carrizo did. Strangely, so did Pablo Rojas Paz. Borges obtained the vote of the only writer among the judges: Eduardo Mallea." José Luis Ríos Patrón, *Jorge Luis Borges* (Buenos Aires: Editorial La Mandrágora, 1955), p. 114.

The fact is that Borges did not present *Ficciones*, as Ríos Patrón would have it, but rather *El jardín de senderos que se bifurcan* (1941), as Rodríguez Monegal states, since *Ficciones* appeared in 1944 (two years after the event in question) and contains the stories collected in *El jardín* in addition to the stories of a second collection entitled *Artificios*. See the detailed bibliography of Borges in Ana María Barrenechea, *La expresión de la irrealidad en la obra de Borges* (Buenos Aires: Editorial Paidós, 1967), pp. 247–56. The English translation of Barrenechea's book is entitled *Borges, the Labyrinth Maker*, ed. and trans. Robert Lima (New York: New York Univ. Press, 1965). The original Spanish edition of *La expresión...* was published in Mexico City: Colegio de México, 1957. [FS & CMZ]

16. A reflection of this episode, carried out with that irony of ironies so typical of Borges (in which there is no lack of joking about himself), appears toward the end of "El Aleph":

> Six months after the demolition of the building on Garay Street, the [publishing house of] Editorial Procusto did not allow itself to be frightened off by the length of the sizeable poem [of Daneri] and distributed a selection of "Argentine fragments" to the bookstores. It is needless to repeat what happened: Carlos Argentino Daneri received Second National Prize for Literature. First Prize was awarded to Dr. [Antonio?] Aita; Third Prize to Dr. Mario Bonfanti [a laughable character of Bustos Domecq]; incredibly, my work *The Gambler's Cards* did not garner one single vote. Once again, envy and lack of understanding had won the day! I haven't managed to see Daneri for quite some time; the newspapers say he will soon regale us with another volume. His exalted pen (not yet benumbed by the Aleph) has been consecrated to the versification of the epitomes of Dr. Acevedo Díaz.

17. It is curious that of the seven writers recalled by Borges, only four of them were contributors to that issue (No. 94) of *Sur*. The following twenty-one names make up the complete list: Eduardo Mallea, Francisco Romero, Luis Emilio Soto, Patricio Canto, Pedro Henríquez Ureña, Alfredo González Garaño, Amado Alonso, Eduardo González Lanuza, Aníbal Sánchez Reulet, Gloria Alcorta, Samuel Eichelbaum, Adolfo Bioy Casares, Angel Rosenblat, José Bianco, Enrique Anderson Imbert, Adán C. Diehl, Carlos Mastronardi, Enrique Amorim, Ernesto Sábato, Manuel Peyrou, and Bernardo Canal Feijoo.

18. Borges and Sábato maintained a brief polemic about aspects of Peronism in three issues of the magazine *Ficción* which appeared in November

1956, and in March and May 1957. The three notes (the first and the third by Sábato; the second, by Borges) are reproduced in Ernesto Sábato, *Claves políticas* (Buenos Aires: Rodolfo Alonso, 1971), pp. 57–71.

19. Sábato's dedication to Borges: "How the world turns, Borges: When I was a boy, during those years that now seem to belong to a kind of dream, verses of yours helped me to discover the melancholy beauties of Buenos Aires: in old neighborhood streets, in the wrought-iron window gratings and cisterns, even in the modest magic that at dusk can be contemplated in some pond in the outer fringes of town. Then, when I came to know you personally, we were able to converse on those Buenos Aires themes, whether directly or under the pretext of Schopenhauer or Heraclitus of Ephesus. Then, years later, political rancor separated us, and just as Aristotle says that things are distinguished by the way they resemble each other, perhaps we could say that men are separated by the very thing they love. And now, as distant as we apparently are (what a strange world this is), I would like to offer you these pages that have occurred to me on the tango. And I would very much hope you're not displeased by them. Believe me. Sabato." *Tango: discusión y clave* (Tango: Discussion and Key) (Buenos Aires: Editorial Losada, 1963).

20. "But Enrique Santos Discépolo, its greatest creator, gives what I believe to be the most heart-felt and accurate definition: 'It is a sad thought which is danced out.'" (Ibid., p. 11).

21. Borges' comments are curious; Discépolo is the composer of some of the most famous and most popular tangos. [CMZ]

22. *El túnel* (translated by Margaret Sayers Peden as *The Tunnel*) (1948) and *Sobre héroes y tumbas* (translated by Helen R. Lane as *On Heroes and Tombs*) (1961). *Abbadón el Exterminador* (translated by Andrew Hurley as *The Angel of Darkness*) was published in 1974, after the recording of these conversations.

23. *Uno y el universo*, Ernesto Sábato's first book (1945), was written after he abandoned his career in science and after withdrawing from public life in 1944. It is a book of personal and philosophical essays; among other awards, it won the coveted Premio Municipal for prose in 1945. [CMZ]

24. Borges translated Arthur Conan Doyle's "The Red-Headed League" as "La Liga de los Cabezas Rojas." It was included in *Los mejores cuentos policiales*, an anthology he compiled with Adolfo Bioy Casares (Buenos Aires: Emecé, 1943).

25. See Jorge Luis Borges, "La poesía gauchesca" (Gaucho-Style Poetry) in *Discusión* (Buenos Aires: Emecé Editores, 1957), pp. 22–24; Elías Carpena, "Defensa de Estanislao del Campo y del caballo overo rosado" (Defense of Estanislao del Campo and the Strawberry Roan Horse), *Bo-*

letín de la Academia Argentina de Letras, XXIV, nos. 91–92 (January-June), 73–109; and "Centauros de gesta: El caballo overo rosado en las dos acepciones de parejero" (Epic Centaurs: The Strawberry Roan Horse in the Two Meanings of *parejero*), *Boletín de los Cursos de Extensión Cultural "Constantes de Hispanidad" del Instituto Argentino-Hispánico* (Buenos Aires, 1965), pp. 3–12. A detailed bibliography is provided by Horacio Jorge Becco, *Fausto*, prologue by Jorge Luis Borges (Buenos Aires: Edicom, 1969).

26. Rafael Hernández, *Pehuajó: Nomenclatura de las calles* (1896).

27. It is one of the illustrations re-done by Dorothy Colles based on Tenniel's drawings for the first edition of Lewis Carroll's *Alice's Adventures in Wonderland* (1865) and *Through the Looking-Glass* (1872). The picture is on page 94 of the Collins edition (London and Glasgow) of 1964.

28. See note 6 of the First Conversation.

29. "Los orilleros" was filmed in 1975, directed by Ricardo Luna.

Jorge Oscar Pickenhayn refers to a statement made by Ulyses Petit de Murat (found in María Angélica Bosco, *Borges y los otros* [Buenos Aires: Compañía General Fabril Editora, 1937], p. 159) to the effect that Borges collaborated with Petit de Murat, the filmmaker, in writing a screenplay many years ago which "someone or other lost." See Jorge Oscar Pickenhayn, *Borges a través de sus libros* (Buenos Aires: Editorial Plus Ultra, 1979), p. 32. [CMZ]

Seventh Conversation

1. Borges is referring to the etymology of the word "Bible." In European languages, the word derives from the Medieval Latin plural form *Biblia* (the same spelling as the singular Spanish term) which in turn derives from the Greek plural form, i.e. "books." [CMZ]

2. Borges' first trip to Israel, at the invitation of the Israeli Government, took place at the end of 1968 and the beginning of 1969. He gave several lectures in Tel Aviv and Jerusalem, and was received by David Ben-Gurion. It was on April 19, 1971, during his second visit to the Jewish State, that Borges was awarded the Jerusalem Prize. The prize had been presented to Max Frisch, Bertrand Russell, and Ignazio Silone in previous years. [CMZ]

3. Borges received an honorary doctorate from Columbia University in 1971. Oxford University awarded the honorary Doctor of Letters that same year. [CMZ]

4. The verse is part of this quartet:

Y transportado al fondo del Nirvana
o, como buen genial, contradictorio,

prosiguió razonando, perentorio,
sin ver, en su razón, razón humana:

(And transported to the midst of Nirvana
or, as a real genius, contradictory,
he continued reasoning, peremptorily,
without seeing, in his reason, human reason:)

Almafuerte, "El misionero," VIII, 1–4, in *Lamentaciones* (La Plata, 1906), p. 45.

    5. The line is:

Do I contradict myself?
Very well then I contradict myself,
(I am large, I contain multitudes.)

Walt Whitman, "Song of Myself," Section 51, third stanza, in *Leaves of Grass*. [CMZ]

    6. León Felipe's version of "Song of Myself" is the book *Canto a mí mismo* (Buenos Aires: Editorial Losada, 1941). It contains an epilogue by Guillermo de Torre.

    Borges did the selection, translation, and prologue for *Leaves of Grass* in Spanish: *Hojas de hierba*, with a "Critical Study" by Guillermo Nolasco Juárez (Buenos Aires: Editorial Juárez, 1969).

    Leandro Wolfson, in his article "Tres veces Walt Whitman" (*Idiomanía*, año 1, No. 5, August 1992, pp. 18–23), carries out a very interesting comparison among the translations of a fragment of "Song of Myself" done by [Álvaro] Armando Vasseur, León Felipe, and Jorge Luis Borges.

    7. Actually, it is the book *Páginas muertas* (Dead Pages), with a prologue by the author and an "Estudio epílogo" ("Epilogue Study") by Borges (Buenos Aires: Minerva, n.d.). Horacio Jorge Becco says it was published in 1928 (*Jorge Luis Borges. Bibliografía total, 1923–1973* [Buenos Aires: Casa Pardo, 1973], p. 20).

    8. Original Spanish:

Cuando la tarde se inclina
sollozando al occidente

These are the first lines of the very long poem, "Santos Vega," included in *Poesías* (1885; lengthened in 1906), Rafael Obligado's only book. These verses are well known to the average Argentine reader.

    9. Original Spanish:

Ocre y abierto en huellas, el camino

separa oscuramente los sembrados.
Lejos, la margarita de un Molino,

From the poem "Paisaje" (Landscape) dated 1916; it appeared in the collection *Campo argentino* (Argentine Countryside), 1920. [CMZ]

10. The Revolt against the Spanish Crown resulting in Independence. [CMZ]

11. It was my foolhardy error to formulate such a grim prophecy. To everyone's benefit, Borges continued writing his literature, which, in turn, and as always, gave rise to a copious production of studies on his work, in Spanish, in English, and in many other languages.

12. Translated into English as *The Book of Fantasy* (New York: Viking, 1988).

13. The following is an English translation of Marco Denevi's "The Master Betrayed":

> The Last Supper was taking place.
> "Everyone loves you, oh Master!" said one of the disciples.
> "Not everyone," the Master solemnly responded. "I know someone who is envious of me and will sell me for thirty dinars at the first opportunity."
> "I know to whom you are referring," exclaimed the disciple. "He spoke ill of you to me too."
> "And to me," added another disciple.
> "And to me, and to me," said all the others (all except one, who remained silent).
> "But he's the only one," continued the one who had spoken first. "And to prove it to you, we shall all call out his name in unison."
> The disciples (all except the one who kept silent) looked at each other, counted to three and shouted the name of the traitor.
> The walls of the city shook with the reverberations, for the disciples were many, and each one had called out a different name.
> Then the one who had not spoken went out into the street and, free of any remorse, carried out his betrayal.
>
> (Jordi Liost, *El Evangelio herético*, unpublished. Translated from the Catalán by M.D.)

Marco Denevi, *Falsificaciones* (Falsifications) (Buenos Aires: EUDEBA, 1966), p. 9. Liost is a fictitious author.

14. Borges' *Discusión* opens with a quote from Alfonso Reyes' book *Cuestiones gongorinas* (Issues about Góngora). The epigraph reads: "This is

what is bad about not sending one's work to the printers: one spends one's life re-doing it." [FS]

Borges' paraphrase of Alfonso Reyes' reasons for publishing one's writings ("one publishes a book in order to leave it behind, one publishes a book in order to forget it") is remarkably parallel with a statement concerning women in Borges' "Los teólogos" (The Theologians): "There are men who seek out a woman's love in order to be able to forget her, to get her off their minds . . ." In *El Aleph*. [CMZ]

Catriel, Cipriano, 4
Cervantes, Miguel de, 4, 22, 96, 133
Chaplin, Charles, 28
Chesterton, G. K., 65, 67, 113, 123
Claudel, Paul, 73, 108
Coleridge, Samuel Taylor, 45, 46
Coliqueo, Simón, 4
Conan Doyle, Sir Arthur, 112,
    113, 114
Conrad, Joseph, 120, 121
Cooper, James Fenimore, 38, 39
Cortázar, Julio, 49, 50, 59
Cromwell, Oliver, 61

Dante, see Alighieri, Dante
Darío, Rubén, 12, 17, 102, 103, 129
Daudet, Alphonse, 35
Debussy, Claude, 26
Della Scala, Can Grande, 72
Dell'Oro Maini, Atilio, 94
Denevi, Marco, 132
De Quincey, Thomas, 67
Díaz, Porfirio, 106
Dickens, Charles, 34
Di Giovanni, Norman Thomas, 29,
    30, 75, 119
Discépolo, Enrique Santos, 111
Donne, John, 5
Dostoyevsky, Feodor, 65, 66

Eça de Queiroz, José Maria de, 23,
    34, 35
Echeverría, Esteban, 33
Eichelbaum, Samuel, 30, 31
Eliot, T. S., 63
Erigena, Johannes Scotus, 72
Erro, Carlos Alberto, 96, 110

Fairbanks, Douglas, 45
Faulkner, William, 50, 118
Felipe, Léon (Léon Felipe Camino),
    127
Fernández, Macedonio, 13, 14, 15,
    79, 80, 92

Fernández de Andrada, Andrés, 56
Fernández Moreno, Baldomero, 30,
    128, 129
Fitzgerald, F. Scott, 118
Flaubert, Gustave, 34, 35
Frost, Robert, 53

Galdós, see Pérez Galdós, Benito
Gálvez, Manuel, 79
García Lorca, Federico, 104, 105
García Márquez, Gabriel, 131
Garcilaso de la Vega, see Vega,
    Garcilaso de la
Gardel, Carlos, 9, 26, 83
Gerchunoff, Alberto, 31
Gibbon, Edward, 108
Girondo, Oliverio, 8
Goethe, Johann Wolfgang, 112, 125,
    126, 133
Góngora y Argote, Luis de, 5, 21,
    103, 107
González Tuñón, Enrique, 19
González Tuñón, Raúl, 19, 29, 30
Grabher, Carlo, 72
Grondona, Adela, 59
Grondona, Mariana, 59
Groussac, Paul, 23, 24, 25, 38, 49, 68,
    95, 96, 129
Guido, Beatriz, 39
Güiraldes, Ricardo, 8, 18, 19, 37, 39,
    82, 104, 106, 129
Gutiérrez, Eduardo, 38, 39, 110, 129

Haedo, Ester (cousin), 87
Hardoy, Emilio, 88, 89
Hardy, Oliver, 28
Hawthorne, Nathaniel, 38, 50
Heine, Heinrich, 69, 126
Hemingway, Ernest, 118, 119
Henríquez Ureña, Max, 57, 129
Henríquez Ureña, Pedro, 54, 55,
    56, 57
Hernández, José, 21, 23, 36, 42, 43,
    110, 115, 116, 129

Vega, Garcilaso de la, 13, 22
Vega, Lope de, 67
Verlaine, Paul, 21, 26
Verne, Jules, 76, 77
Virgil, 70

Wagner, Richard, 26
Wells, Herbert George, 21, 44, 63, 67,
    76, 77, 132

Whitman, Walt, 127
Wilde, Eduardo, 127, 128
Wilde, Oscar, 114
Woolf, Virginia, 50

Yrigoyen, Hipólito, 88, 89, 90

Zemborain de Torres, Esther, 94, 95

CPSIA information can be obtained
at www.ICGtesting.com
Printed in the USA
LVOW08s2028151116

513041LV00001B/1/P

9 781589 880603